Small Bandsaw Techniques

Peter Bishop

D1494777

The Crowood Press

First Published in 1997 by
The Crowood Press Ltd
Ramsbury, Marlborough
Wiltshire SN8 2HR

British Library Cataloguing-in-Publication Data
A catalogue reference for this book is available from the British Library

ISBN 1 86126 054 7

Line illustrations by David Fisher.
Photographs by the author unless otherwise credited.

Typefaces used: text, New Baskerville and Garamond; headings, Optima Bold.

Typeset and designed by
D & N Publishing
Membury Business Park
Lambourn Woodlands
Hungerford, Berkshire.

Printed and bound by Paramount Printing Ltd, Hong Kong.

ACKNOWLEDGEMENTS

A large number of people and organizations have helped with the provision of information, detail and general support. The listing below, I hope, covers most of those who have contributed in some way. To any I have inadvertently forgotten, please accept my apologies.

Zach Taylor for his advice at the outset, continued support throughout the writing of this book and for providing the foreword.

Richard Keen of Tewkesbury Saw Company Limited for his patience, provision of facilities and sources of information.

Geoff Dutson from the Hereford College of Technology, where I gained my qualifications many years ago.

The Axminster Power Tool Centre who provided one of their excellent machines.

Darkin & Company (Saws) Limited for the provision of material on different types of saw blades.

Slack Sellars & Company Limited for a mass of information on saw blades.

My old friend Peter Smith who provided me with information from his workplace.

BriMarc Associates for details of and a kit to braze silver steel blades.

Forester for furnishing the photographs of their portable 'Jacko' horizontal bandsaw.

The Science and Society Picture Museum for supplying figures 2, 3 and 4 in the Introduction.

Excerpts from BS 4411:1969 (1986) are reproduced with the permission of BSI. Complete editions of the standards can be obtained by post from BSI Customer Services, 389 Chiswick High Road, London W4 4AL.

James Jones & Sons Ltd, for providing information and the last five photographs in the introduction on their high-yield sawmills.

Good Bros (Timber Merchants) Ltd, for allowing me to wander all over their sawmill facility.

CONTENTS

FOREWORD

I feel an immense pleasure in being asked to write the foreword to this most necessary book. The subject is a machine which I have come to respect and rely on as a luthier and a woodworking journalist. Few machines have had such an impact on small workshop practice than the small bandsaw. As a general-purpose saw it has great facility and with its special functions offers sawing operations unique unto itself.

Those unique qualities do not include restriction of the bandsaw to its expert followers; on the contrary, its simple function encourages the tyro with little experience to approach it with confidence. It is possible to become proficient on the bandsaw without ever having used any other kind of saw, powered by motor or by hand.

Every kind of woodworking area, from the joinery trade through furniture production and the specialized trades of shop-fitting and boat-building has come to depend on this machine, and since manufacturers have made the small bandsaw available it has come home, literally, to the domestic workshops of the hobby craftsman.

Add to the basic function of the bandsaw some imaginative ingenuity with jigs and tricks and its range may be extended to include sophisticated joints and fancy profiling. Many would-be craftsmen limited to hand tools would not dare to embark upon some projects that, given access to a bandsaw and sound technical advice, become straightforward with a built-in promise of success.

Best it is, of course, when the novice who wishes to go beyond the normal sawing operations is accompanied by a craftsman already experienced, successful and enterprising.

Regardless of your level of skill, I will wager that there is information within these covers that will help improve your relationship with your bandsaw. So, take it into your workshop, stand in front of your bandsaw and read on.

Zachary Taylor
Harrow 1997

INTRODUCTION

When I was first asked if I would like to write a book on bandsaws, I thought: 'Yes, I can do that – no problem.' After all, I have been using (and no doubt abusing) bandsaws of various shapes and sizes for nearly thirty years. However, as time went by and my research progressed, I started to realize that I knew less than I had thought about bandsaws and all the associated paraphernalia. Probably akin to the modern motorist, I knew how to drive the thing but had forgotten what went on under the bonnet. I have consequently gone through a sharp learning curve. Although I knew the basics plus a bit, the people who have helped with material on blades, machines and techniques have had a resounding effect upon my knowledge level. I only hope I am able to capture and impart some of that information. I apologize if that sounds pompous – it's not meant to. I hope you will have as much enjoyment reading this book as I have had in its preparation.

I love working with wood, especially British hardwoods. This book is about cutting and working with all types of timbers using small bandsaws. Wood is frequently misused, and will probably continue to be so, but it is the only material I know which is both forgiving and naturally renewable. Creating a piece of furniture or whatever from such a resource can give so much pleasure to both the maker and user – long may that continue.

The content of this book is aimed at the serious user of the small bandsaw, be he tradesman or DIYer. My definition of a 'small' bandsaw is loosely intended to include those machines that generally use a blade 1in (25mm) wide or less. The book is deliberately focused upon what to look for and expect from a machine, blade type, care, maintenance and techniques. It does not set out to be an engineering discourse. I hope to provide enough technical information for operators to fully utilize their machines. There are no real projects to complete, but demonstrated functions and detailed explanations are employed which aim to benefit anyone using a small bandsaw. Although we will be focusing our attention on discussing the use of bandsaws for cutting timber, these machines have a much wider use. They are used extensively in other industries and some of these alternative uses will be outlined briefly. It would be remiss of me not to give some history and background on bandsaws here at the very beginning. It will help to understand their development and wider capabilities outside the scope of this book.

THE DEVELOPMENT OF BANDSAWS

Bandsaw evolution is allied to the development of saws in general. Prior to mechanization, the best known method of cutting large pieces of timber was using the 'pit' saw technique. In the seventeenth and eighteenth centuries most large villages and estates had saw pits but no one to operate them. Stocking up with raw materials they would await the arrival of itinerant gangs of sawyers who travelled the countryside. In larger towns and cities there were permanently staffed pits. The

Fig 1 Pit sawing. The sawyer on top, the 'topman', is the one who guides the cut through the log.

object to be cut was placed over the pit, with one sawyer standing on the topside – known as a 'top-man' – and another down in the tip – called the 'pit-man'.

Using a double-handled saw, the top-man and the pit-man would alternately push the blade through the cut. The top-man would have to guide the saw – he was the only one who could see where it was going. Even today, pit-sawing continues in some developing countries. Environmentalists favour the practice as the only way in which to convert logs into lumber without the introduction of, as they see it, destructive mechanical methods. Pit-sawing must have been a particularly onerous job and fortunately was eventually superseded by powered reciprocating and frame saws, driven initially by water.

Around 1800, circular saws were in the early stages of development. I believe Sir Marc Isambard Brunel patented a circular saw in 1806. Simple water power transmission to a drive-shaft made these saws

Fig 2 A model of an old reciprocating saw circa 1900. *Note that the blade is driven up and down to produce an action similar to a hand saw. (Reproduced with the permission of the Science & Society Picture Library.)*

Fig 3 Model of a circular saw bench, circa 1860. *(Reproduced with the permission of the Science & Society Picture Library.)*

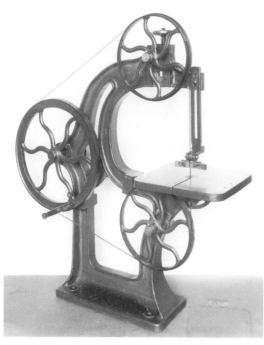

Fig 4 A hand-powered three-wheeled small bandsaw, circa 1885. (Reproduced with the permission of the Science & Society Picture Library.)

extremely popular. Various blade sizes were available, proving especially useful for veneer cutting at that time. Today in just about every serious woodworking establishment circular saws are still to be found. Circular saws with large-diameter blades were popular in log conversion mills for many years. However, they have long since been superseded by high-tech bandmills.

At about the time circular saws were being developed, the first attempts at designing and making bandsaws were underway. Initially these machines were simple unguarded wheels with a jointed band of toothed steel wrapped around, hence the name 'band' saw. At first breakages and poor quality steel were serious problems, and it was the mid-nineteenth century before brazing steel and steel technology could produce a reasonably successful blade. Within a few years the

bandsaw was established as the primary machine for cutting wood. Compared with the circular saw, the bandsaw was more economical to use, the width of cut being much finer, and it could also cut much larger sections.

By the beginning of the twentieth century 'bandmills' for converting logs into lumber were well established. The basic technology remains the same today, but with many refinements. The thickness of blade, type of steel, tooth design and width of cut etc., have all developed tremendously, improving both yield – the amount of usable material cut from logs – and production rate. It is hard to believe these will continue to be improved upon, yet no doubt they will be.

MODERN PRACTICE

In most cases, bandsaws manufactured today cut vertically, with the blade action from North to South. The blade can be configured to the left- or right-hand side. Some bandsaws are designed to cut horizontally, cutting East to West, or vice versa. Large versions of the horizontal machines can be found in log conversion mills, the most common being self-propelled portable machines. This type of bandsaw is ideal for small estates, farms and foresters who are offering a cutting service. Usually driven by a petrol engine they have the ability to go just about anywhere the towing vehicle can take them. They are today's version of the pit-sawing teams who once travelled the countryside.

Broadly, there are three different types of bandsaw in use today; we are interested in the small vertical bandsaws that do not regularly use blades over 1in (25mm) in width. They may have two or three wheels, none of which exceeds 30in (760mm) in diameter. Larger sizes generally fall into the band 'resaw' range and tend to be used for

Fig 5 Loading an oak log onto a portable self-propelled horizontal bandsaw. The saw is driven by a small engine mounted at the top right-hand corner of the machine. (Reproduced with the permission of Standrange Ltd.)

Fig 6 The portable horizontal bandsaw in action. The machine is slicing a board about 1in (25mm) thick off the oak 'baulk' moving, as it cuts, towards the camera. (Reproduced with the permission of Standrange Ltd.)

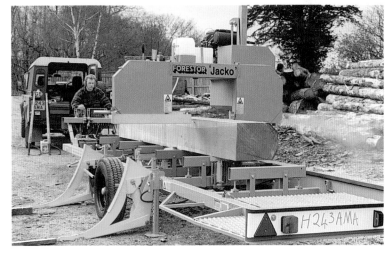

cutting lumber into another size from the original piece, hence the name resaw. Most resaws will have a minimum blade of 1in up to 6in (25mm–150mm) and twin wheels up to around 50in (1270mm) or so. Finally we come to the largest machines used for converting, or 'breaking down' logs into lumber. In the trade they are referred to as 'headrig' saws. These are really large beasts, with blades up to 40ft (12m) long and 16in (400mm) wide. Some older specialist machines were designed to have teeth on both sides so that the operator could cut the log both ways as it passed the bandsaw on its carriage. Even today, blades are available with two cutting edges for specialist applications.

To confuse the above classification slightly, bandsaw blades fall into two categories. A 'narrow' blade does not exceed 2½in (63mm) in width and a 'wide' blade is one that is over 3in (75mm) in width. Narrow blades normally run on pulley wheels that are flat and have a rubber 'tyre' or 'band' wrapped around them. Wide blades run directly on metal wheels that are 'crowned'; this difference will be discussed later.

CONVERTING LOGS

The conversion of logs into lumber can be a highly technical process today, in which bandsaws play a major role. The objective is to maximize the 'yield' – the amount of usable material – from each log as it goes through the mill. In a fully integrated softwood mill, nothing is allowed to go to waste. Bark is stripped off and sold through garden centres as a mulch and weed inhibitor. Sawdust is collected along with chips produced from unusable offcuts from the logs. This is then sold to other mills for the production of composite boards such as chipboard or fibreboard. The lumber itself will be cut to predetermined commercial sizes.

In a hardwood mill the bark and sapwood is cut off in slabs during the conversion process and sold as firewood or cheap fencing. Sawdust is also collected. Because of the differing types of wood being cut, this sawdust is normally unsuitable for the composite board market. It may therefore be sold as litter to go under poultry, horses or other farm animals. The lumber from hardwood mills will generally be cut to order, with any falling pieces cut to standard sizes for fencing, flooring beams or other uses.

The most skilled job in any sawmill is that of the sawyer who operates the headrig

Fig 7 The in-feed end of a typical UK home-grown hardwood conversion mill. In this case oak logs are being loaded onto a cross-transfer feed system at the front end of the band mill. (Photographed at Good Bros (Timber Merchants) Ltd.)

Fig 8 The business end of a bandmill. Fitting a new blade to the headrig saw; this is not one of the largest! (Photographed at Good Bros (Timber Merchants) Ltd.)

saw. The initial cuts will determine the profitable yield from each log. A mixture of judgement, experience and equipment is needed to optimize the amount of usable lumber produced. In a typical UK hardwood mill, logs are fed into the bandmill. Depending upon the sophistication of the operation the logs will be scanned electronically or visually for shape, defects or – the bane of every sawyer – metal particles. If metal is encountered during the sawing operation, it can easily strip away all the teeth from the blade. Blades are changed fairly regularly before they become too blunt; failure to do so will produce poorly cut material.

Once fed onto the automated carriage, even large logs weighing many tons can be turned and angled mechanically to the most suitable cutting position. The sawyer will decide which is the best way to initiate the cutting sequence. As the log goes through the initial cutting process, it is taken to the vertical cutting edge of the blade on a carriage and the first slab is removed. The next sequence of cutting will remove slabwood or boards from another side of the log.

When two opposing sides have been dressed to produce the desired even thickness, the log will be rotated. The first edge-cut is then made along one side. The

Fig 9 Where to cut? The headrig sawyer is of key importance when it comes to deciding what can be cut from the log. This bent log has to be cut to produce a beam. (Photographed at Good Bros (Timber Merchants) Ltd.)

Fig 10 First cut. The automatic carriage has been adjusted to align the log to best advantage. The hydraulic 'dogs' at the back of the log on the carriage can be moved to achieve this. (Photographed at Good Bros (Timber Merchants) Ltd.)

Fig 11 Final cut. The beam is cut and drops onto the out-feed automatic rollers to be taken away. (Photographed at Good Bros (Timber Merchants) Ltd.)

operator may decide to cut off more slabwood before the final production commences.

Once the object piece or pieces have been cut, they will exit the mill via roller tracks, after cross-cutting if necessary. If large slabs are produced they may be fed to the resaw for further conversion travelling via the roller tracks and some cross-transfer arrangement.

At the opposite end of the spectrum comes the fully integrated softwood conversion mill. As already mentioned yield is of critical importance along with speedy efficient cutting. In Europe raw materials will be sourced from managed and natural forests. In the UK the largest provider is the Forestry Commission followed by private growers. We are all familiar with those vast new forests passing us by on the motorways, especially in Wales and Scotland. Fast growing species are predominant, various Spruces, Pines and Larches, all suitable for construction, structural and fencing use. We will never be self-sufficient but whatever is grown here will reduce our reliance upon imports.

When softwood reaches maturity in a managed forest it is likely that a whole block will be ready for harvest at the same time. Everything will be cut and cleared.

Tops and branches are left behind helping to provide cover for the saplings that will be planted on the site. The logs will be loaded onto lorries and deposited at the sawmill for conversion into lumber.

Before the main sawing process gets underway the logs will be cut to economical regular lengths. Following this they will be loaded onto the automatic in-feed end of the mill. On a cross transfer chain fed system the logs will be stacked ready to enter the first cutting cycle. They will be kept in a supply stream to ensure the sawmill is continuously working. The first cuts, butt reducing, are made with twin bandsaws cutting parallel and to each side of the log.

The whole process flows from one machine to another automatically. In the background of the picture showing the logs awaiting first cuts can be seen some returning on the other side. These have been fed back up the mill to a cross transfer arrangement to enter the next cutting cycle which trims the other outer edges off. The squared log, or baulk as we should call it, will undergo further processing to produce lumber.

The culmination of all this activity produces large volumes of standard sized timber. The bandsaw has once more played the key role, converting logs into lumber.

Fig 12 Softwood logs being unloaded and stacked ready for conversion. (Reproduced with the permission of James Jones & Sons Ltd.)

Fig 13 The initial cross transfer arrangement feeding logs to the first bandsaws. Note the returning logs on the other side heading for the second series of cuts. (Reproduced with the permission of James Jones & Sons Ltd.)

Fig 14 A log approaching the first pair of bandsaws to reduce the butt to a regular width. (Reproduced with the permission of James Jones & Sons Ltd.)

Fig 15 Once squared, the baulk is then cut into lumber. (Reproduced with the permission of James Jones & Sons Ltd.)

Fig 16 Lumber produced from a softwood conversion mill in Scotland. The material with plastic sheeting over it in the background is kiln dried. (Reproduced with the permission of James Jones & Sons Ltd.)

WARNING

MANY OF THE DIAGRAMS AND PHOTOGRAPHS IN THIS BOOK SHOW THE MOVING PARTS WITH CASES AND GUARDS REMOVED; THIS IS FOR THE CONVENIENCE OF SHOWING YOU, THE READER, CLEARLY SOME DETAIL. DO **NOT** ON ANY ACCOUNT EXPOSE YOURSELF TO THIS DANGER – BANDSAWS CAN BE LETHAL MACHINES.

---

one

STARTING OUT

This chapter sets out the key design features associated with small bandsaws, their configuration, cutting capabilities and so forth. It should be helpful to those who already have a machine and wish to understand further its limitations and versatility. Perhaps it will be most useful to those who are about to purchase a bandsaw. It sets out the main design points and features to look for when making your investment.

BASICS

You are likely to come across three different types of small bandsaw: bench-mounted two- or three-wheeled, stand-mounted two-wheeled, and, finally free-standing, fully encased, heavy-duty models. Each type has its own attributes and limitations which we will progressively discuss.

Small bandsaws have certain common features, although these are not always in the same position. Most of the readily available small bandsaws have a right-handed configuration. The cutting side when facing the machine from the material in-feed end will be to the right-hand side. I am not aware of any UK manufacturers who currently offer a left-hand alternative, but I have seen them in the past. Some US machines are configured to the left-hand side, and no doubt they are available should you specifically require one. If you already have one then by now you will have got used to feeding your material from a different side. Photographs etc., in this book, relate to right-handed machines.

FRAMES

One of the key factors affecting performance is the design and construction of the bandsaw frame. A loose floppy frame will not allow the machine to cut efficiently. This would be the case regardless of the guide system and blade choice. There are three ways in which manufactures strive to attain the stability required. The smallest machines tend to have lightweight cast alloy frames. In-built strengthening within this structure involves thicker cross-bracing and raised channels. To help avoid any flexing between the top and bottom wheels this type of model should be firmly fixed to a bench or purpose-built stand. Smaller machines are more than adequate for most hobbyist workshops. However, do not expect to be able to cut large sections continuously on them because they were not designed for that purpose. I have to say at the outset that I am not too keen on these very small machines, especially the three-wheeled models. In my opinion they are not man enough for most of the work they are likely to encounter during their working lives. I also believe they are not really built for longevity. If considering buying a bandsaw or upgrading, I would go for a larger more substantial machine every time.

The medium- to heavy-duty machines will adopt one of two ways to form a rigid framework. In the first instance a welded frame is used as the basic structure, added to which are the coverings, casings and anchor points for the attachments. This type of small bandsaw should come ready

Fig 17 Typical small bench-mounted three-wheeled bandsaw. This one has the advantage of also having a sanding disc.

equipped with a separate floor-stand, or may have an integral casing. The strength here is derived from the box sections used in construction. If these are too light, there is likely to be some flexing in use and operation. Most medium- and some heavy-duty machines currently on the market will be constructed in this way.

Most older-style and industrial-type heavy-duty machines tend to be constructed using one-piece castings, or a combination of casting and welding. These will be the most stable machines. Providing they have been correctly engineered it is unlikely that you will find much movement within their frames.

If you do have any movement in the frame of your small bandsaw, it will probably lead to the blade being twisted slightly

out of true while it runs. This will lead to additional stresses being set up, which may result in the blade fracturing prematurely. To check for this, physically grasp the machine top and bottom wheels, and see if you can detect any movement. If you can, your machine will need to undergo some strengthening work; if you are simply considering purchase, avoid it altogether. When buying, do not be shy. You should ask your supplier to set up the machine for a test run and let him feed some thick material through to see how it goes. Watch carefully as the timber is fed – see if any flexing is visible. Have a go yourself and see if you can feel any 'give' during the cutting action. If you do you will know not to touch that model. When setting out to purchase a new machine your

Fig 18 A small two-wheeled bandsaw
mounted on its own stand.

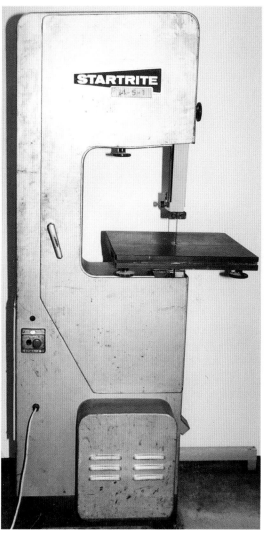

Fig 19 A fully encased free-standing
small bandsaw with two wheels.

personal budget will no doubt play a
major part in the decision-making. In
addition to this, however, give some consideration to the types of material you are
likely to be cutting. If you believe a lightweight bandsaw will be adequate for your
work load then so be it. If heavy cutting is
on the agenda, do not expect the smaller
machines to perform as efficiently as a
larger one should.

WIDTH AND DEPTH OF CUT

It may be important to you to be able to
accommodate certain widths or depths of
cut from your bandsaw. The restriction on
throat-width will be directly related to the
size of wheels on your small bandsaw.
With a two-wheeled machine it cannot
exceed a factor somewhat slightly below

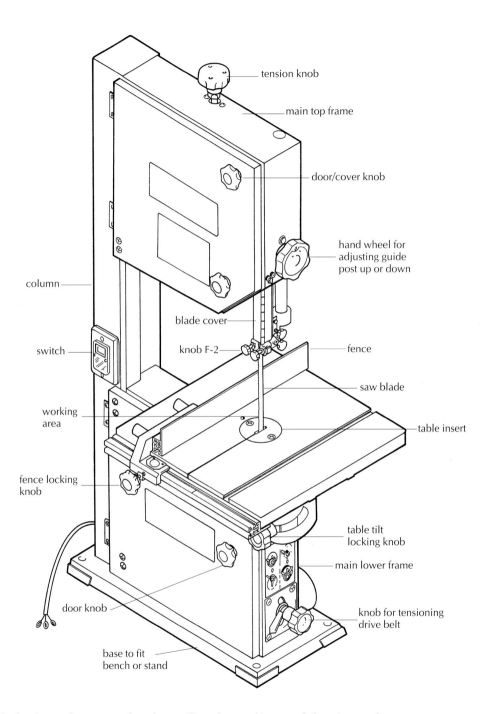

Fig 20 Getting to know your bandsaw. (Based on a diagram belonging to the Axminster Power Tool Centre).

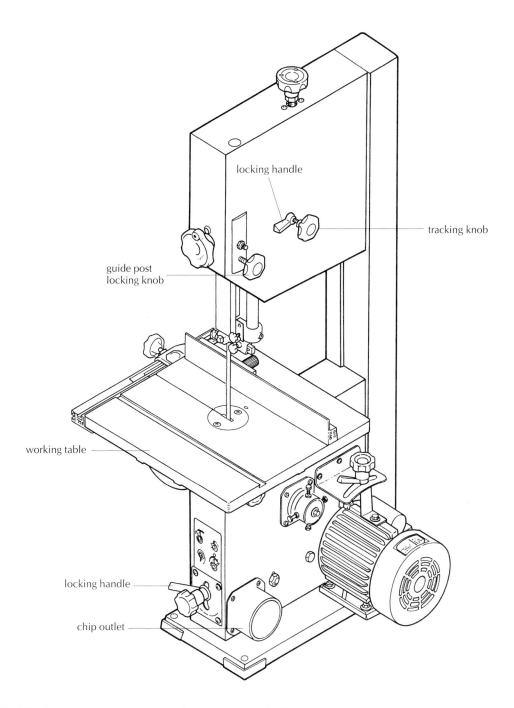

Fig 21 Getting to know your bandsaw, continued. (Based on a diagram belonging to the Axminster Power Tool Centre.)

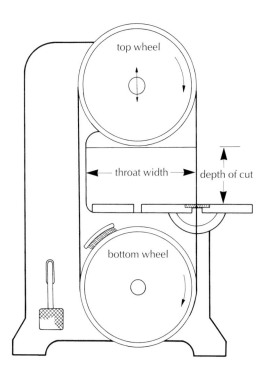

Fig 22 Internal view of the two-wheeled APTC small bandsaw showing a welded frame.

Fig 23 The points at which the throat-width and depth of cut are measured.

Fig 24 Internal view of a three-wheeled machine showing the frame-strengthening to improve rigidity.

*Fig 25 The throat-width of
a three-wheeled small bandsaw is not restricted to
casing or wheel size.*

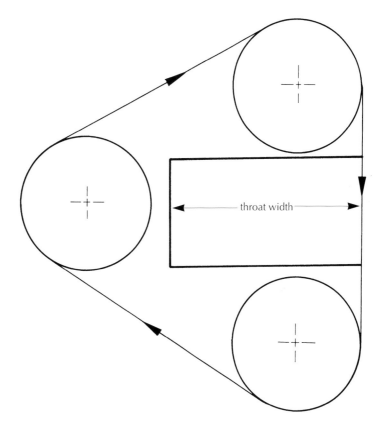

throat width

*Fig 26 Common above- and
below-table guide assembly.*

Fig 27 Typical top-adjustable post and guide assembly.

throat. In addition to this, some two-wheeled small bandsaws are classified by the size of their wheels. In most instances it is down to the individual maker how they differentiate between models. Alternatively, the depth of cut will determine the size. The restricting factors are the position of the main saw-table and the height at which the saw guides can be set. Some industrial machines may have the facility to increase the depth of cut by rising part of the top frame structure, thereby increasing the cutting capacity. In the unlikely event that you come across one, remember that you will probably have to make your own blades up to suit the varying sizes!

GUIDES

We will be discussing in detail the critical importance of setting the guides correctly in the next chapter. If you are setting out to purchase a small bandsaw it will be useful to understand some of the necessary features. The purpose of the guide assembly is to support and guide the blade as it makes the cut. Additionally it should avoid placing unnecessary stresses upon it that may lead to fracturing and breakage.

There are two assemblies: one fixed in place below the table and another, adjustable to suit the workpiece, above the table. The components of each individual assembly are made up of supports. These are for each side of the blade and at the back of the blade. All must be adjustable. Generally today the two side supports are manufactured from hard wearing synthetic materials or, more commonly on the older machines, wood. The back support needs to rotate with the blade and should be in the form of a 'thrust' bearing with a hardened steel disc face. Check closely that both assembly sets have plenty of adjustment for wear on the side blocks.

the wheel diameter. After taking into account the blade-guards and casing the throat will probably be somewhere around ½–1in (12–25mm) narrower. The exceptions are the three-wheeled models. Their configuration allows a wider throat measurement to be achieved.

If width of cut is important, then three-wheeled machines offer an alternative to larger two-wheeled bandsaws. This will depend upon the type of work you will be doing. The width of throat tends to be used as the measuring tool for the smaller saws. A 10in (250mm) machine should have the corresponding width of

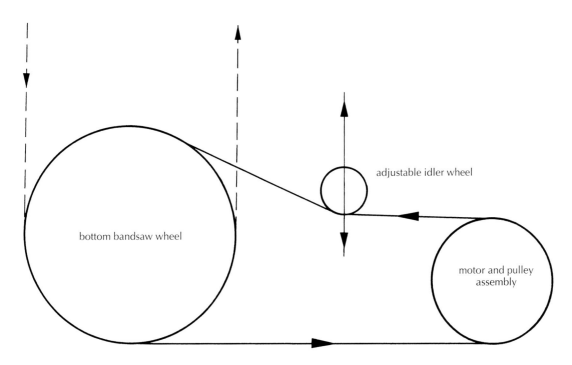

Fig 28 Tensioning the drive belt with an adjustable idler wheel.

The back thrust bearings must move back and forth to accommodate varying blade widths. The top assembly also needs to be freely adjustable for height. It is usually fitted to a sliding post. Make sure that it is able to move down close to the table and also up towards the top casing. This latter movement provides the maximum depth of cut capacity for the machine.

POWER AND TRANSMISSION

In all but a few isolated instances, power is provided to the machine via either a single-phase electric motor run from a domestic supply source, or alternatively an industrially rated three-phase motor with its own dedicated supply. The three-phase supply is generally only an option if it is already in place, although it is possible to get phase 'converters' that will up-rate single-phase domestic supply to three-phase. I am no expert on these gadgets and believe that for most small bandsaws single-phase will be more than sufficient. If given the choice between, say, a machine driven by a ½hp or 1hp motor, go for the bigger one if you can afford it. It is always better to have some spare power in hand rather than make the motor struggle. When cutting thick and hard material you will need to feed it through slowly. An under-powered machine will become very frustrating when the cutting action slows down or stops! It may also be advisable to avoid any machine that has a direct drive from the end of the motor spindle – direct drive machines like these may burn out their motors quicker through abuse or misuse. A belt drive acts like a slipping clutch – if the blade stops for any reason the belt should slip.

The drive belt from the motor pulley to the bottom wheel of the small bandsaw may be tensioned in various ways. The motor may be mounted on a pivot with a slide assembly. Tension in this case is generated through hand pressure being applied and then locking the motor in place. An alternative method is for the motor to be fixed to the frame or body of the machine and for there to be an adjustable idler wheel to apply the tension. The belt runs around this wheel. This is then wound up or down on a slide to apply the necessary pressure to the drive belt.

One other commonly used technique for applying tension to the drive belt is to use the weight of the motor itself. The motor is slung under the bottom bandsaw wheel on a tray that is pivoted on one end. Some sort of mechanism is used to lift the other end. When the support is taken away the weight of the motor takes up the slack in the belt allowing the transmission of power to the bottom wheel.

Most of us fail to but, if you can remember, try to release the pressure from the drive belt when your small bandsaw is not in use. This will prolong the life of the belt and will also avoid undue pressure being applied to any of the bearing assemblies. In addition to the tensioning arrangements already mentioned many small bandsaws will be driven at one or two speeds via a vee belt and pulley assemblies.

SPEED

Speed is measured in feet per minute (FpM), and refers to the distance the blade travels within that period. The FpM value is dictated by the ratio between the motor drive pulley and the driven bandsaw wheel. Somewhere between 2,000 and 3,000 FpM is more than sufficient for general use. When cutting thick stock, this should be increased if possible – the faster the blade goes, the quicker the sawdust is

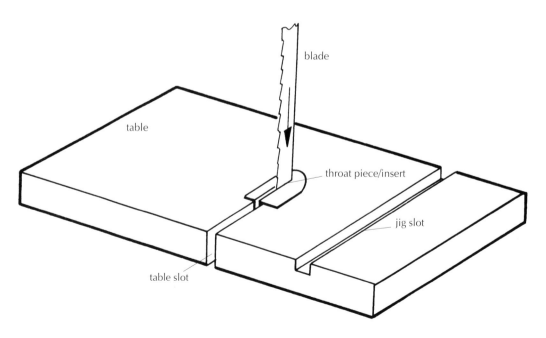

Fig 29 Typical small bandsaw table set up.

Fig 30 Typical table slot and throat arrangement.

cleared away. The feed speed at which the workpiece proceeds through the machine is more critical. If you go too fast for the blade to clear away the waste sawdust, it will become clogged. This leads to the blade possibly burning its way through rather than cutting, and it may even break. In all instances the practised operator will be able to balance between the FpM of the machine and the feed speed of the material being cut.

BANDSAW TABLES

The saw table surrounds the blade and provides the platform from which the workpiece enters the cutting cycle. Most small bandsaw tables feature a slot through which the blade is threaded to mount it on the wheels. In some instances, part of the table will be hinged to swing out of the way or it may actually lift off to allow for this access.

An enlarged throat is cut into the metal table to avoid accidental damage to the blade teeth and to facilitate loading. The throat-piece is positioned in the table at the point in which the blade passes through it.

These throat-pieces should just slip out when changing blades. Sometimes they are held in place with a couple of screws; the blade may pass through all right, but it is normally easier to remove them. If the throat-piece wears, it can be usually be replaced by purchase through your

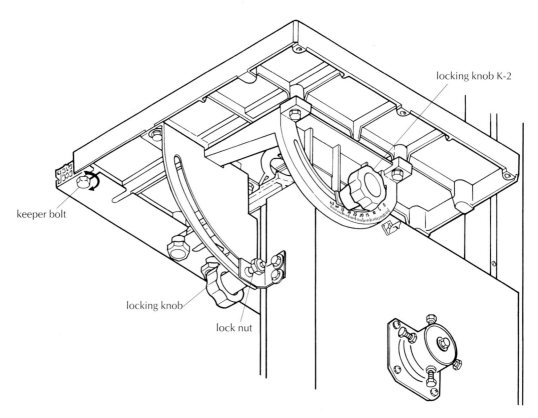

Fig 31 Details of a tilting table assembly. (Based on a diagram belonging to the Axminster Power Tool Centre.)

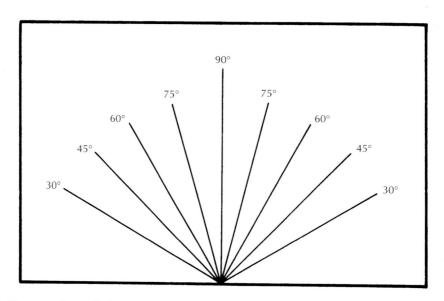

Fig 32 Home-made angle jig.

supplier. If none are available you will be able to make your own from plywood or other composite materials. When fitting your own, be sure to make the throat-piece fit level with the table of the saw – slightly beneath is better than over, which may distort the cutting action. On the front of the table there should be an adjustable fence – hopefully, calibrated. This is used for rip-sawing parallel widths through the machine. Additionally it is usual to find a jig or mitre slot to the right-hand side of the blade. This is used for cutting various angles and some joints using an attachment that we will discuss in more detail later.

Small bandsaw tables will generally also have the facility to tilt. This is a great asset if you wish to cut an angled section of wood parallel to the saw cut. Tables that have this facility are mounted on matching semi-circular trunnions. These allow the whole thing to tilt while keeping the throat centrally aligned with the blade. They are usually calibrated and fitted with a locking device. In most cases it is likely that the maximum angle of cut achievable is 45 degrees. This will be achieved by tilting the table away from the column of the machine.

If perhaps your table can tilt but it is not calibrated, you can make up your own simple protractor jig. Mark the degrees out on a card or light metal alloy rectangle. Make sure that the bottom edge – the one that sits on the table – is flat and straight. Mark as many angles as you might require from a central point. When you want to set up the machine to cut angles using this jig, start by loosening the table locking nuts. Then place the protractor card behind the blade, tilting the table to the desired angle. Follow this by locking the table in place. With any of these operations, always cut a piece of waste to make sure the angle, etc., is cut as required.

WASTE

It is important that the waste sawdust can easily fall away or be ejected from the inside of the bandsaw casing. Check that there are no ledges where build-up is likely to occur. If you think there is likely to be a problem it will be advisable to avoid buying that machine. If you already have the problem, it is worthwhile considering fitting some sort of waste extraction.

If you are considering buying, take an overall look at the potential machine. Will it be easy to get the blades on and off? Are the guards and covers sufficiently well made to do their job? Where are the lubrication points? And so on. The main thing will be the overall impression of sturdiness and stability. Do not buy a Rolls-Royce if a Mini will do but do not expect the Mini to cut as well as the Roller! If possible insist upon a test-run using the machine yourself, you will soon get a feel for it. If the supplier has not got a machine available ask where you can go to try out somebody else's. Run it up and cut a few pieces, if it 'shakes, rattles and rolls', avoid it. Make sure that you feel comfortable with the machine you buy. If you are not relaxed, it is likely that there will always be hesitation in use leading to poor operator performance and quality of finish.

two

BASIC OPERATION

One thing we must all remember when operating a powered machine of any description is to treat it with respect. It always amazed me that my wood machining tutor many years ago had lost several fingers from each hand! An excellent instructor, and very experienced, he freely admitted that familiarity had been the main cause of his injuries. I took note, and to date have kept a full set! Because safety is important I have highlighted here a few pointers that you should bear in mind if you wish to remain undamaged.

• Read the instructions before you start; after work has started it may be too late.
• Always switch off the power supply at the mains before setting up, adjusting or doing anything that might bring parts of your body in proximity to moving parts.
• Make sure all the safety guards are in place before you turn on your bandsaw.
• If you have long hair, tie it back out of the way.
• Do not wear loose or frayed clothing that may be pulled into the machine; do not wear gloves.
• Keep your work station clean – offcuts, rubbish and dust will hinder smooth operation.
• Wear goggles, industrial glasses or a visor.
• Use a dust mask – some timber particles are carcinogenic.
• Keep you hands and fingers away from the saw blade – use a push-stick.
• Make sure you have set the machine on firm ground, that it is stable and does not wobble about.
• Check that the correct blade tension is

applied, that it is tracked and that the guides are set accurately.
• Do not use damaged or badly worn saw blades.
• Make sure you cannot be distracted when operating the machine, shut the door and keep the kids out.
• When you finish, turn off the power supply and release the tension from the saw blade.

These are just a few initial pointers that will be covered in more detail in Chapter 7.

FITTING THE BLADE

Always ensure you have the right blade length for the machine. The bandsaw will have been designed for a particular length of blade with some allowance for tensioning. You will not get a blade on that is too short but probably will be able to fit one that is too long – do not! Switch off the machine before you start.

Undo the covers and guards, removing or swinging them out of the way. You may have to take off part of the saw table or remove the sliding gear for the fence. Loosen the guides above and below the table making sure they will not foul the blade. If the blade is coiled, be careful when releasing it – try wearing gloves to protect your hands. Undo the retaining pieces, hold at arm's length turning your face away before you let two of the three coils go. (I did not do this on one occasion, and ended up with a cut nose and upper lip the day before an interview with a prospective client.) It is a good idea to uncoil the blade away from any machinery or metal parts. This will help to avoid losing the edge from any of the teeth before you even have it on the machine. The blade should release itself into its natural shape. Check to see if the teeth are running in the right direction. Often when uncoiling blades they have a tendency to undo in the wrong way but it is not a problem to put right. Just grasp the blade firmly on both sides and twist inside out. When you have released the blade, check for fractures and signs of stress or damage before you put it onto the bandsaw. If new it is likely to be well oiled or greased. Wipe this off before mounting by holding a rag in one hand and running the blade through it with the teeth going backwards, to avoid damaging your hands or snagging the rag.

Fig 33 A machine with guards, covers and fence assembly swung clear to give access for blade fitting.

With the tension wheel slackened off, start by slipping the blade onto the bottom wheel first. This should avoid the odd instance when you may not have quite got the blade on the top wheel. It might drop off onto your back or neck as you struggle to get it on the bottom wheel. With the bottom in place wrap the blade onto the other one or two wheels until it is loosely in place. Most small bandsaws have flat wheels and are set up so that the wheels are directly lined up in the same plane. The top wheel will have a facility to cant backwards or forwards to adjust the tracking. Most machines feature the top wheel canting and remaining so as part of the design.

It is a possibility that on some older machines the wheels may be 'crowned' rather than flat. This is more generally found on larger bandsaws using wider blades over 1in (25mm) width. It is a device that helps 'track' the blade. The principle is simple, exerting forces on the blade from both directions makes it 'ride' on the top of the crown, wherever it is situated upon the wheel. Only part of the blade will be in contact with the wheel which may lead to some blades wandering during operation. As a rule I find flat wheels most suitable for the small bandsaw. They provide better control once they have been tracked correctly.

Most flat wheels will be fitted with a rubber or composite material 'tyre' or band. This helps maintain friction whilst the blade is being driven and protects it from contact with the metal wheels. Some manufacturers recommend the blade be tracked in the centre of the wheel and others with the teeth hanging over the leading edge. Read your instructions to establish which you should follow. If I have a choice I tend to hang the teeth over the front edge. This is simply because, in my opinion, it prolongs the life of the tyre. With small and medium blades under ½in (12mm) this is impossible and they should be tracked to run on the tyre.

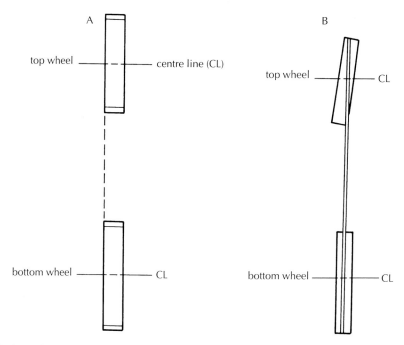

Fig 34 A: in-line wheel assembly. B: tilting top wheel for tracking the blade.

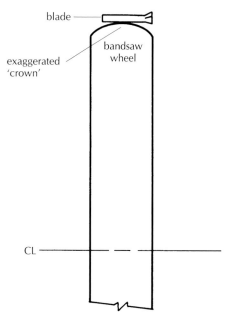

Fig 35 Blade 'riding' the top of a crown wheel.

TRACKING

Having fitted the blade to the machine it will now have to be tracked and tensioned to ensure it runs true, stays on the wheels under power and cuts efficiently. The blade needs to be tracked first. This also entails applying tension simultaneously and the guides should be well clear of the blade. Determine if the blade is to run in the centre of the wheels or overhanging the front edge. Adjust the top wheel to take up any slack so that the blade does not flop around. Rotate the top wheel manually and watch how the blade runs, apply more tension as you go. It will soon become apparent which way the blade is running, forwards or backwards on the wheels. Using the top wheel cant mechanism make the adjustments necessary to run the blade in the desired position, increasing the tension to the correct setting. If not under the correct tension the

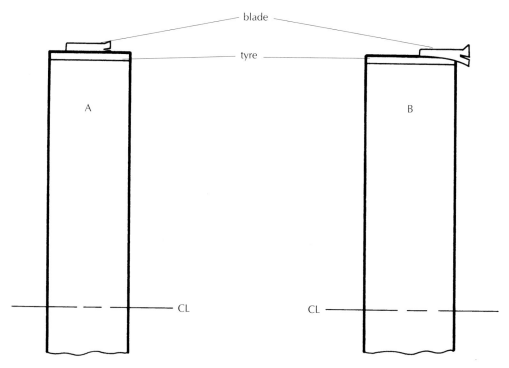

Fig 36 Flat bandsaw wheels. A: blade is centrally tracked. B: blade is tracked to overhang the front edge.

tracking will not be complete. Any further adjustments will probably distort the way in which the blade runs.

Many machines will have the tracking and tensioning adjustment knobs and mechanisms adjacent to one another. Turning one will alter the angle of the top wheel and the track of the blade, tightening the other increases the tension. Some tracking devices are located directly onto the top wheel. Adjustments are made in the same way by rotating the central knob.

If you have difficulty tracking your blade it is possible that one or a combination of external factors will be causing this. Overtensioning, which is discussed shortly, may put extra strain on the top wheel, preventing it from running true. If the blade has not been jointed correctly this may tend to throw the blade one way or the other. In addition the blade may also have been distorted during one of the hardening

processes. When rotated, the blade will tend to track back and forth on the wheels. It may be that the bearings are wearing on one or both of the wheels. If you think this is the case release the tension, remove the blade and check for movement. Each blade runs in a slightly different plane, therefore move the guides back out of the way and reset them at every change.

TENSIONING

To obtain accurate and smooth cutting the correct tension must be applied to the blade. Placing the blade under tension avoids movement and flexing when the blade is in use, helping to keep it straight. It is normally a simple process to adjust the tension but if this is not done correctly it can have a significant effect on performance.

31

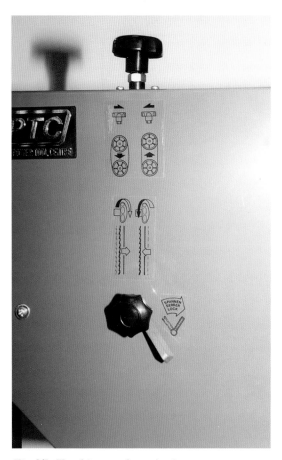

*Fig 37 Tracking and tensioning
adjustment knobs with locking lever.*

Read the instruction manual to determine how tension should be applied to your machine. Under-tensioning will result in poor blade performance and the blade will veer off the line of cut when pressure is applied. Over-tensioning can result in permanent distortion of the saw frame and an inability to track the blade correctly.

There are a number of techniques for determining if the right tension has been applied – each manufacturer seems to have his own variation. Some machines will have an indicator that points at a scale of blade widths. One old machine of mine shows the blade width in a little window.

With others, you simply tighten the tension until a certain amount of sideways movement is achieved. Yet another may have a lamp that lights up when the correct tension is reached.

Whatever else, uniform tension needs to be applied, usually through adjusting the upper wheel. In addition to this constant tension the machine needs to be designed to absorb any shocks. This was achieved on older machines by the use of counterbalanced weights to both create the tension and absorb the shock. Modern machines generally adopt a spring mechanism.

Experience will eventually tell you how much tension is required for the differing width and thickness of blade and the type and sizes of material being cut. Initially follow the manufacturer's instructions and tension the blade accordingly. Spring mechanisms accompanied by a scale are common, but if the tension is not released when the machine stands idle, over time they will become inaccurate. In these cases you may need to adjust the tension of a narrow blade up to the next size on the scale.

Tightening the blade until a restricted amount of sideways movement is achieved is another common technique. One manufacturer uses the side casing as a guide. If the blade can reach this with reasonable pressure it is about right; if it goes easily, it is too slack. Others will claim a sideways deflection of 1, 2 or even up to 5mm is sufficient. Experience gained with cutting different materials will help you decide how much deflection is appropriate. One of the easiest ways, with practice, is to strum the blade like a musical instrument's string and listen to the result. Using the back edge (do not cut your fingers on the front), hook a finger over it and let it go. Listen to the note it makes. If clear and sharp, you have probably got the right tension; if dull and flat, it may be under- or over-tensioned. Listening to the changing notes while increasing the

Fig 38 Spring tensioning mechanism on a three-wheeled machine.

tension is best if you can manage it. Try winding the tension up and strumming or plucking the blade with your free hand – you will soon hear the difference. As the tone changes you will also be able to tell if you go over the top. Remember that different width blades will make different notes. Narrow blades will have a higher note, unlike the bass notes produced by a wider one.

Blades that are over-tensioned have too much pressure applied to them and will tend to break sooner. Conversely it is important to have the correct tension applied to avoid flexing during the cutting sequence. An under-tensioned blade will appear to have a will of its own. If attempting to cut a straight line through stock up to about 1in (25mm) thick the blade will wander off in one direction or the other. As it moves out of line, this will increase the tension, and the blade will then wander

back, or break. When cutting thicker stuff the effect can be more dramatic. As the blade increasingly takes up the slack tension within the stock itself, this produces a barrel-like cut.

If the blade is correctly tensioned, you should enjoy a fair degree of continuity of cut while in operation. Having tensioned the blade, do not just carry on regardless. In operation you may need to stop and alter it. If cutting a large amount of thick hard stuff the blade is bound to heat up. As this occurs it will expand, becoming longer, and some of the tension will be released. If work is to continue in this way, stop the machine and re-tension the blade. If you have left the machine under tension for some time without using it, there is a fair chance that the tension will have altered and will need adjusting. Your own experience will eventually lead to correct tensioning.

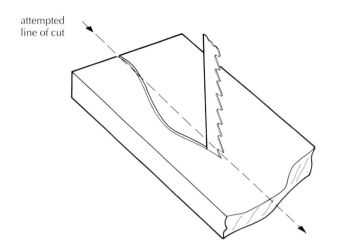

attempted
line of cut

*Fig 39 A 'wandering' cut.
Not enough tension may
allow the blade to wander
away from the line of cut.*

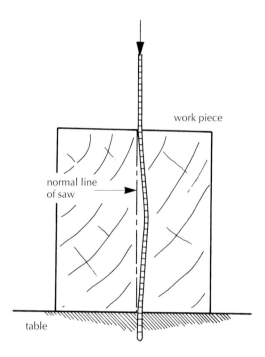

work piece

normal line
of saw

table

*Fig 40 A 'barrel' cut. A blade that is
too slack may increase its tension
within the workpiece, not cutting true,
so producing a barrel cut. At worst the
blade will move so much that it is
unable to go back and may break. (Try
as I could I was unable to produce
either the wandering or barrel cuts to
photograph!).*

SETTING THE SAW GUIDES

Having loaded the blade, tracked and tensioned it, the only major adjustment remaining is to set the saw guides. Even if all other factors and settings are correct, poorly adjusted guides will lead to a loss of performance. Typically, guides on small bandsaws are made of metal, wood or synthetic fibre blocks. They are adjustable to support the sides of the blade with a thrust-bearing arrangement positioned behind the blade.

Normally there are two assemblies. One static set of guides slung below the saw table and another set above the table on a sliding height column or post. In both cases the blocks and thrust-bearings must be fully adjustable. This is to allow clear movement away from the blade during changing and movement back when it is in place for support. They will also need to have adjustable lateral movement forwards and backwards to accommodate differing widths of blade.

Adjusting the top assembly to suit the differing thickness of timber being cut is important. The whole thing must move up or down a post. The objective is to give

34

Fig 41 Guide-holder adjustments. (Based on a diagram belonging to the Axminster Power Tool Centre.)

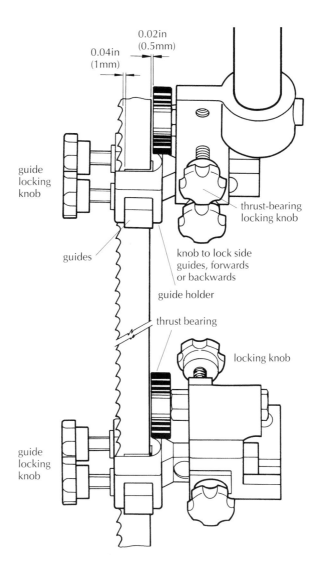

0.02in (0.5mm)

0.04in (1mm)

guide locking knob

thrust-bearing locking knob

guides

knob to lock side guides, forwards or backwards

guide holder

thrust bearing

locking knob

guide locking knob

close support above the material being cut. This will help to avoid the blade deflecting or being placed under undue pressure. Ideally, about ¼in (6mm) clearance above the workpiece is sufficient. This gap should be enough for you to see any marks that you may be cutting to. As an added bonus it stops your fingers getting too near the blade.

To set up the side blocks correctly, the blade must already have been tracked and tensioned. All cover-guards need to be removed to allow free access to the gear for adjustment. Loosen the block-retaining grub screws, bolts or whatever. Move each side block up to the blade making sure that it does not quite touch. A gap of ³⁄₁₀₀₀in (0.076mm) is about right – the thickness of a cigarette paper if you have one. Do it by eye if you wish. Alternatively, try a mechanic's feeler gauge, used for plug gap setting. This should ensure the support is equal on both sides. If pressure is exerted unduly at one or more points on

Fig 42 Above- and below-table guide assembly – guards and cases removed.

When feeding a workpiece through the small bandsaw the blade has a natural inclination to move backwards away from the pressure being applied. The thrust bearings are there to support the blade and stop that action. They should be adjusted to sit about $^{15}/_{1000}$in (0.38mm) behind the back edge of the blade. When the sawing action commences, the blade moves back slightly. It should connect simultaneously with both the bearings causing them to rotate. This rotation helps to reduce heat build-up caused through friction. When the cutting action ceases, the blade tracks back to its original position and the thrust-bearings come to rest. If this does not happen, the tracking or the thrust-bearings need adjustment. Make sure that both top and bottom bearing assemblies are lined up. If one is slightly proud undue pressure will be exerted on the blade causing it to bend between the two contact points. Any incorrect adjustment will reduce the life of the blade. Some manufacturers attach a plate to their machines giving instructions on how to set up the guide assemblies.

Thrust-bearings need to be set correctly and kept well lubricated. If you fail to do this they may become damaged, or cause damage to the blade through overheating. If the blade gets too hot it can suffer metal fatigue that will lead to fracturing and failing. Typically the bearings will become clogged and eventually seize up. When this happens the back of the blade will start to wear grooves in the bearing face. With damaged thrust-bearings like this, the blade will always tend to slip back into the groove, eventually cutting right through it.

Rounding the back of the blade may help to avoid damaging the thrust bearings. This may be useful if the machine is to be used over prolonged cutting periods. It stops the blade digging into the bearings and also assists when cutting smaller radiuses. To achieve this, first equip yourself with some

the side of the blade it may cause deflection. This leads to poor cutting performance and a shortening of blade life. The side blocks must be positioned just behind the saw teeth providing support to the blade body. There should be a facility for the whole assembly to be moved backwards and forwards locking in place. Depending upon the width of blade I tend to leave a gap of around $^{15}/_{1000}$–$^{20}/_{1000}$in (0.38–0.5mm). This setting is past the gullet depth and will avoid the blocks becoming damaged during the cutting action as the blade moves slightly back to come in contact with the thrust-bearing.

safety goggles and a fine-cut file. Bring down the top guide assembly close to the table, allowing enough space to see and manoeuvre the file. With the tracking device, set the blade to run back against the thrust-bearings; this will help to stop the blade coming off. Start the machine and using the file, gently take off the corners, rounding the back of the saw blade. Do not apply pressure to the extent that the blade overheats, and be very careful – remember what we said earlier about fingers! Rounding the back of the blade should go some way to stopping it digging into the thrust-bearings. As a bonus, the blade will cut curves better and may run somewhat quieter. If contemplating long runs, it is useful to have a can of penetrating oil handy. Give the thrust-bearings a quick squirt every now and again – it will help to avoid them seizing up.

Side block guides can be made up from various types of materials. Many older machines use wood, some use fibrous synthetic blocks and others metal. All will claim that their particular type of block is more efficient than others and will no doubt extend blade life. I am sure there must be some merit in these claims. The key issue is not the cooling of the blade during use, but why it might be getting hot in the first place. If the blade is tracked,

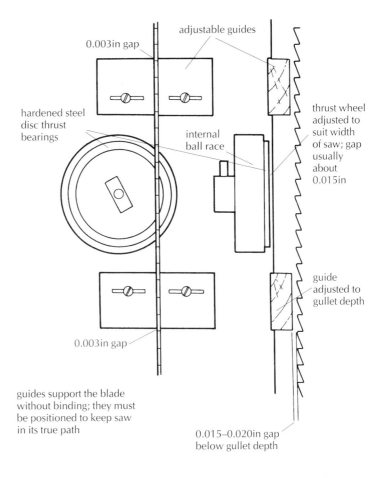

0.003in gap

adjustable guides

hardened steel disc thrust bearings

internal ball race

thrust wheel adjusted to suit width of saw; gap usually about 0.015in

guide adjusted to gullet depth

0.003in gap

guides support the blade without binding; they must be positioned to keep saw in its true path

0.015–0.020in gap below gullet depth

Fig 43 Small bandsaw guide settings.

tensioned and guided correctly, there should be little overheating. If it does get hot, look for the fault in one or a combination of the set-up factors.

LEVELLING THE TABLE

Having got your blade set up, it is as well to check that the bandsaw table is set correctly to it to ensure a square cut. Most tables will be able to tilt on trunnions to allow for angled cuts; we discussed this earlier on in Chapter 1. To set the table square, initially look for and find the levelling bolts. Normally located under the inner bottom side of the table, typically they are bolts that can be adjusted and locked off in place Once the bolts are set, the table can be returned to the level every time after tilt-cutting without further adjustment.

Ensure the blade is tensioned and tracked first then, using a square, alter the table levelling bolt until it fits evenly against the body. With the table levelled, lock the bolts off and tighten the trunnion slides.

Having levelled the table, the throat-insert in the middle should have enough clearance around it to allow the blade to run freely. If the table is to be used in tilted mode you will need to bevel the throat-insert's bottom edges away from the blade to allow free movement. If the throat insert is wood or plastic then clearance need not be too much. If a metal one is used it is advisable to increase the clearance to avoid the risk of damaging the blade teeth. If you can, it is a good idea to use wood anyway and make up your own as you need them. Using the old one as a template you should easily be able to cut and shape a new piece to fit. Be sure to make it flush with the table surface or slightly depressed; a proud insert will distort the cut.

IN GOOD HEALTH

Always remember to have the blade covers and guards in place before you start the machine. Having nicked my own fingers a few times I now use a 'push-stick' whenever possible. They are easy enough to make and help to keep the soft bits away from the blade.

Make the push-stick to suit your own hand, increasing or decreasing the angle accordingly. If you make it long enough to start you will be able to re-shape the business end whenever it has (inadvertently!)

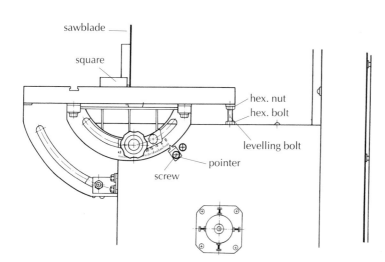

Fig 44 'Squaring' the table. (Based on a diagram belonging to the Axminster Power Tool Centre.)

made contact with the blade. This is a most useful tool and I always have two or three around the workshop for use on the other saws and planes.

I was taught that a tidy workplace helped to create tidy work and vice versa. I have always been rather fastidious about this and probably tend to go over the top a bit. I do, however, believe that it is very important to clear waste away before it fouls any moving parts or gets in the way of a clear run at whatever you are doing. Make sure you can access and turn the workpiece easily around the machine at all the points you are likely to want to reach. This is basic good housekeeping. Clear away the falling pieces before they touch the blade and are kicked at you or fly through the workshop. Clean your glasses or goggles before and during the cutting sequence – it is surprising how quickly they will gather dust and obscure your vision. I always wear a dust mask when sawing. I never cease to be amazed at how much dust and dirt collects on them, and you do not want that down in your lungs. Most of these pointers are common sense. Just be careful and you will have many happy hours sawing away.

MAINTENANCE

Your machine's instruction manual should cover in detail its maintenance requirements but I thought it would be useful to highlight a few points at this stage. It is always good practice to check regularly that all the moving parts and fittings that need to move can do so freely. Remember to turn the power off at the isolation box before you start.

Cutting wood will tend to produce resins and deposits on any parts of the machine that come into contact or are adjacent to this action. Those especially affected will be the blade, wheels and guides. With the

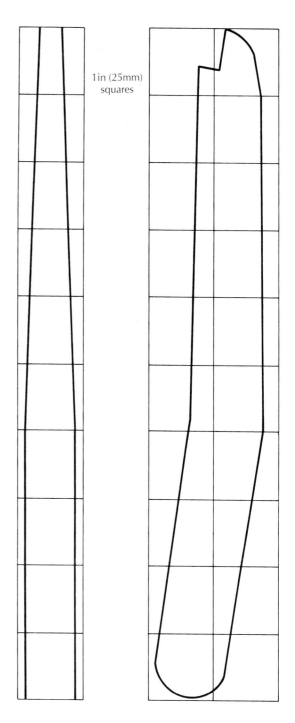

1in (25mm) squares

Fig 45 Plan of a 'push stick'.

Fig 46 Adjustable cleaning brush on a small bandsaw's bottom wheel.

blade off the machine, soften any resin deposits with turps, white spirit or something similar and wipe off the residue. The wheels will attract the deposits mainly because sawdust is trapped between them and the blade. The bottom wheel tends to be worst affected as it is below the table, where most of the sawdust drops. You should find an adjustable cleaning brush situated by the bottom wheel that will help to keep some of the deposits away. If for some reason this brush is not fitted or has been taken off, it is worthwhile considering putting a new one on.

To fit a new brush you assess where it should go, making sure it will not foul any moving parts. If, inevitably, there has been a build up of resin, the wheels will need cleaning. Try first with an alcohol-based fluid, softening the deposits and wiping off. If this fails, you will need to be a bit

more aggressive and use sandpaper. Choose a fine grit, wrap it around a flat block and rotate the wheel by hand applying the sandpaper and block to the tyre. If the wheel is not designed to have a tyre fitted you should be able to clean the deposits off with a cleaning fluid as above. If not, try scraping them off, but be very careful not to damage the wheel surface.

Dust and dirt will affect the guide blocks and thrust-bearings. Make sure that the bearings have free movement and lubricate with a penetrating oil, clean deposits off the blocks and replace as necessary. Check and oil the top guide assembly post. Will it come down low enough to guard your fingers? You should regularly check the blade for fractures or signs of stress. Lightly oil all the moving parts associated with the table. Make sure the table fence can move freely and that the table can tilt fully through the angles to left or right. It is a pain if you find the table has ceased to move when you want to use this facility.

Check that the table is square to the blade, sometimes chips will get under the levelling bolt after tilting, hindering its correct seating. Oil all other moving parts, including lock knobs and levers. Try not to get oil on the table because it will mark your workpiece and be difficult to get out. Look for grease nipples on shafts and bearing housings. These are there for a reason and should be lubricated regularly. It is all a lot of common sense and good practice. A well-maintained machine coupled with the correct set-up will perform so much better than a neglected one.

THE CUTTING EDGE – BLADES

In the introduction I briefly mentioned the development of steel and jointing techniques for bandsaw blades. Today there are many and varied types of blades available. It could possibly be argued that the blade is the most important part of the whole machine, providing construction has followed good engineering practice. As long as stability and rigidity are in-built, guides and pulleys aligned and drive speed correct, there is little that can affect the performance of the bandsaw apart from the blade – excluding, of course, the operator! In this chapter we will discuss the differing types of blade commonly available, tooth design, making up blades, maintenance and performance. In addition we will briefly cover specialist blades for other applications. Although it is covered in some detail, blade design, style and detail is a specialist subject. Always seek the advice of your supplier, especially when contemplating something outside the norm.

BASICS

Understanding some common jargon is necessary when first looking at blades. Extracts from BSI 4411: 1969 (1986), Specification for woodcutting bandsaw blades, have been included in Appendix 1.

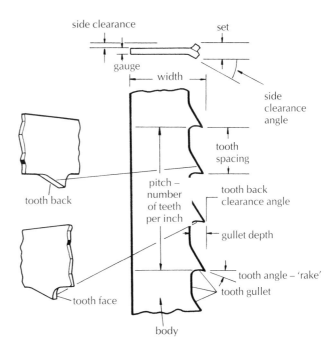

Fig 47 The main features of a small bandsaw blade.

The 'body' of the saw blade is the strip of steel from which it is made. The 'width' of the saw blade is determined by measuring from the back edge of the blade to the front edge of the saw tooth. The 'back' of the blade is the part that is in contact with the thrust-bearings on the saw guidance system. The thickness of a saw blade is described as its 'gauge'. Generally, the thicker and wider the blade, the stronger it should be. It also becomes less flexible and suffers premature breakages if tensioned around smaller bandsaw wheels.

Teeth are ground or cut into the leading edge of the saw blade. An example of a double-edged blade is shown later in the chapter. Each tooth is made up of various components. The 'pitch', or number of teeth per inch, (tpi), will determine the type of material that can be cut with a particular blade and will affect the speed of cut of the workpiece.

Additionally, tooth spacing will affect the surface finish. A greater tpi value gives a smooth finish, or 'fine' cut, fewer teeth produce a rougher surface, or 'coarse' cut. Tooth rake angle and the tpi value help to determine the 'gullet'. This should have a rounded bottom, to avoid stress leading to breakage. It is also the vehicle by which the waste sawdust is removed from the cut. On most small bandsaw blades, teeth are set alternately to each side. This produces the side clearance, creating the 'kerf', thus allowing the blade to cut and operate efficiently. The leading edge of each tooth, the 'point', suffers most of the hammering and wear during the cutting cycle. The 'rake' angle determines how sharp this point is.

THE CUTTING EDGE

Tooth design is a key factor in relation to the efficiency of blade operation. Most small bandsaw blades have teeth designed for rip sawing, because this is the most common use for them. If the machine is to be used for cross-cutting, or surface quality of the final cut is crucial, then careful choice of blade should be exercised. Additionally the type of tooth can be varied for efficiency if cutting hard or soft materials.

The first thing to understand is the relationship between the size of tooth and the tpi value. A large-toothed saw has fewer tpi than a small-toothed saw – each has its own applications. My blade supplier has a golden rule for general cutting; you should always have at least two or three teeth 'in the cut' at any one time, up to a maximum of, say, 6 tpi. With very thin material this may prove difficult. The quality of surface finish will probably be poor and require cleaning up afterwards.

If the machine can be operated at a faster speed, this should indicate that a smaller tpi value can be employed. Alternatively the speed at which the workpiece passes through the machine can be increased. Experienced operators will be able to 'feel' when the machine is struggling to cut; in these circumstances they will ease-off the feed rate. The depth of gullet will also determine how quickly the workpiece can be cut. The purpose of the gullet is to remove the waste wood from the cutting edge, taking it away to allow free access for the leading cutting edge.

Large-toothed saws with fewer tpi will have bigger gullets, allowing for better

Fig 48 Standard tooth form.

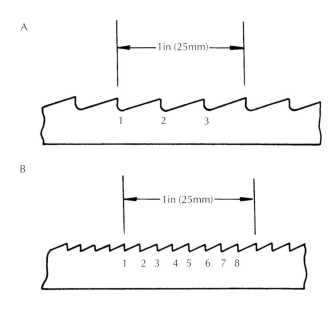

Fig 49 A: 3 tpi for fast ripsawing on materials that are not too hard. This is a 'coarse' cutting blade with large gullets. B: 8 tpi for finer cutting and use on harder materials. A fine cutting blade with small gullets.

waste removal from the cut. If the gullet is too small or the workpiece is forced through the machine too quickly it will fill up and affect the cutting action of the blade. Only experience will give you the required knowledge to understand when to slow down or speed up the feed rate of the workpiece. As a rule cutting thin or hard material requires more tpi than if you are cutting thick or soft stuff. Ideally you want to be able to feed the material through the machine at a comfortable rate, allowing each tooth to enter the cut smoothly and cut equal amounts away.

To allow for the blade to move freely and work efficiently during the cutting action teeth are set wider than the gauge of the blade body. This overall width of the cut, the 'kerf', is the difference between this and the body producing 'side clearance'. Small bandsaws tend to use 'spring-set' blades. Alternate teeth are bent or sprung to one side of the blade or the other, thus creating the kerf. There are variations on the theme, but spring-set saw blades appear to be the most popular.

The amount of set is usually determined by the thickness of the body and the size of teeth. A thick body with few tpi will have a greater set than a thin-bodied saw with more teeth. Manufacturers tend to set saws at about 25 to 30 per cent of the body thickness. If you are using blades that can be re-sharpened and set, this can be varied to give greater side clearance. This practice will allow for cutting tighter radiuses, but it will cut away more material. I shall be discussing the ratios between width of blade and cutting radius in more detail later in the chapter.

The angle and shape of the cutting teeth will have an impact on the blade's performance. In the UK, 'standard' blades are usually produced with a rake or 'hook' angle of 90 degrees and a gullet angle of 60 degrees. This configuration has been tried and tested over very many years and is more than suitable for most wood-cutting activities. On this type of saw blade, the tooth face is set at an angle of 90 degrees to the saw body. It is then said to have a 'zero degree rake'.

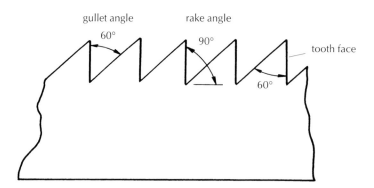

Fig 50 Standard teeth with zero degree rake.

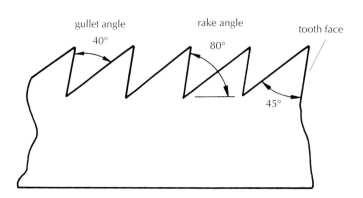

Fig 51 Hook teeth with 10 degree rake.

In some instances the face can be angled forward, producing a 'hook' tooth, known as a 'positive angle blade'.

The hook-toothed blade is more commonly used for cutting metals, with an angle of hook ranging from 5 to 10 degrees. Standard teeth cut more evenly using a scraping action, requiring a proportionally greater amount of feed pressure for them to perform correctly. The hook-tooth is more aggressive, its leading-edge shape helping to pull it into the cut. It cuts faster and with less pressure but the finish tends to be rougher.

There are a whole range of tooth shapes, or 'forms' as they are correctly known. Their position on the cutting edge will influence the performance and finish achieved on the workpiece. Increasing the tpi value on a standard blade may improve the finish quality, but conversely the blade may overheat if the workpiece is fed too quickly.

The standard blade is ideal for most applications, but if you want to cut quickly and continuously a 'skip' tooth blade might be better suited. Designed as an extremely efficient cutting tool, the skip blade is used mainly for cutting softer metals. One of its disadvantages is that the finished surface produced is fairly coarse. Because every other tooth is missed out, the gullet is larger, therefore less heat is generated in use. This should help to extend the life of the saw. Using a skip saw blade to rip down the length of the grain is fine, but trying to cross-cut across the grain

Standard Tooth Form
For general cutting applications of all ferrous materials. The extensive range of tooth pitches from 4 tpi to 32 tpi, cover the full range of applications.

Skip Tooth Form
For non-ferrous metals, softer materials and larger sections. Also for cutting wood. Widely spaced teeth provide extra chip clearance, flat gullets increase band rigidity and act as chip breakers.

Hook Tooth Form
For non-ferrous materials and larger sections. Positive rake angle allows fast cutting at reduced feed pressures. Ideal for the cutting of work hardening alloys, such as stainless steel, where the positive rake angle reduces heating effects at the cutting edge.

Variable Pitch Tooth Form
For pipe, tubing, structural and interrupted sections. Variable pitch also helps to break up harmonic vibrations, dampening noise levels and giving a longer blade life.

Positive Rake
Available in 2 tpi, 2/3VP and 4/6VP. The positive rake angle results in improved cutting of work hardening steels; for example, stainless steel, Nimonics and Ni-Cr alloys.

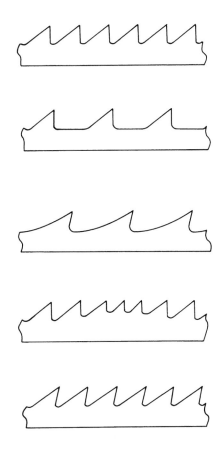

Fig 52 Speed saws. (Based on a diagram belonging to Slack Sellars & Co. Ltd.)

will lead to the wood fibres being torn out.

We have already discussed the hook-tooth design but it is worth mentioning that this particular form of tooth design is particularly useful if you are cutting green, wet, wood. Because of the deeper, more rounded gullet shape it is able to hold more waste material as the blade cuts through the workpiece leading to less likelihood that the blade will clog. Any reduction in clogging will reduce the amount of heat generated and extend the blade life.

Different manufacturers produce their own variations and claim they are superior to other blades. The most common tooth form in woodworking is the standard shape, followed by the skip-tooth and then the hook-tooth.

BLADE BODIES

The bodies of small bandsaw blades are made up from a variety of differing types of steel depending upon the end use and the size of machine on which they are to be used. A blade's area, along with the sharpness of the teeth will determine how long the blade will efficiently last. Over tensioning and therefore applying too much stress in use, forces the steel blade around the wheels, leading to fatigue. When a blade breaks in use we all tend to think it is because we have hit a defect, applied too much pressure, or something similar. In all likelihood the damage and failure due to fatigue was done some time before and it was only the final straw that eventually broke the camel's back. Cutting timber is certainly less stressful than cutting, say, steel, but you should try to remember to cut hardwood at a slower rate than softwood. Do not apply too much side pressure. For cutting timber the most popular bodies available are 'silver steel' and 'flexi-back' blades.

Silver steel blades are produced from rolled spring steel and are generally silver in colour, hence the name. Because they are not heat-treated the teeth and body of the blade have the same hardness. This means they can be re-sharpened using a file.

These blades are more flexible, because the steel is softer. Conversely this adversely effects the cutting life, the tooth loses its edge quicker. Of course they do have the added advantage of being able to be re-sharpened. If a break occurs, silver steel blades can be re-jointed, providing the remaining length is sufficient to go round the pulley wheels. This type of blade tends to be used by the user who enjoys sharpening, setting and jointing his own blades. The steel can be purchased in coils, cut and jointed to suit individual requirements. I guess that even short lengths have been jointed to make up a full-size blade, but care should be exercised. Too many joints may weaken the blade and affect its efficiency.

Using silver steel blades in hardwoods tends to blunt the blade and reduce its cutting ability quickly. In some cases it is possible to have the saw-tooth tips hardened to increase their life. These blades are not commonly available and are difficult to re-sharpen. In most instances they have been replaced by flexi-back blades.

The most commonly used small bandsaw blade found in the wood industry is the carbon steel, flexi-back blade. Steel strips with an increased level of carbon content, to make the tip harder when treated, are rolled out to a predetermined size. The teeth are then milled and set, following which the whole thing is heat treated to harden the teeth. The cutting edge on this type of blade lasts a lot longer than silver steel and the body is still reasonably flexible.

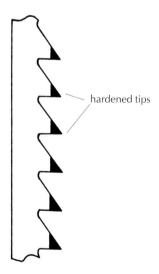
hardened tips

Fig 53 Silver steel saw blade with body and teeth of the same hardness.

Fig 54 Silver steel saw blade with hardened tooth tips.

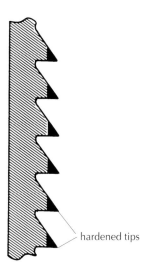

Fig 55 Flexi-back saw blade with flexible back carbon steel body and hardened tooth tips.

Unfortunately, the flexi-back blade cannot be re-sharpened with a file, because of the hardening process. The cost of machine sharpening of such a blade far outstrips its value, therefore once blunt it is best disposed of. It is fairly easy to differentiate between these flexi-backed blades and the silver steel type, as they are 'blued' to a deep blue or black finish. Normally they are priced in such a way that in a production environment, it is difficult to justify the additional time for jointing and re-sharpening, unlike the silver steel blades. This aside, the flexi-back blade tends to be the most popular one in use.

Amongst the wide variety of blades available for different applications there is another carbon blade, the 'hard-back'. This blade has all the attributes of the flexi back but the back edge has been hardened to help it resist extreme pressures. It is used in the metal cutting industries, where extreme feed pressure may be applied as the workpiece is fed through the machine.

This pressure leads to blades breaking frequently from the back. Because of their reduced flexibility, these blades are most suited to large-wheeled bandsaws. They are an expensive item compared with other wood-cutters and rather an extravagance. The flexi-back blade is usually more than suitable for most purposes. I recommend that you should not be exerting excessive pressure to the extent that you need a hard-backed blade.

In addition there is a whole raft of specialist saw blades, many of which may be used to cut wood. The 'bi-metal' blade has a narrow strip of high speed steel jointed onto the cutting edge of the blade body. Normally this strip of high speed steel. is about half the depth of the teeth, which are formed after the jointing process.

Bi-metal blades are used in the metal cutting industry and really are too expensive to consider for cutting timber. In addition to the bi-metal blades there are many variations on the theme, created by tipping a blade with harder materials such as

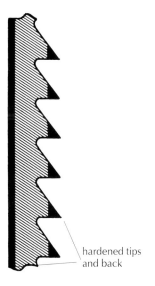

Fig 56 Hardened back carbon saw blade with hardened tooth tips.

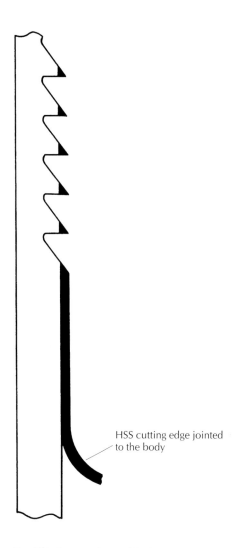

HSS cutting edge jointed to the body

Fig 57 Bi-metal saw blade with high-speed steel (HSS) tooth tips.

tungsten carbide, stellite steel or diamond compounds. The tungsten carbide and stellite tipping techniques are used a lot in hardwood mills on band re-saws and head-rig saw blades. Duration of the tooth sharpness is extended, but the sharpening and replacement of tips takes longer. There is a wide variety of blades available for different applications.

FACTORS AFFECTING OVERALL PERFORMANCE

In addition to the type of metal from which the blade is produced consideration should be given to the thickness and width of the blades. Wrapping a bandsaw blade less than 8ft (2.4m) long over two or three small wheels and applying tension is likely to produce fatigue. Most small bandsaws drop into this range. Care and thought must be given when choosing the right blade for your machine and also the job you intend to use it on. A fatigued blade is not easy to spot unless you are looking for it. Tell-tale cracking to the back edge is the most obvious sign. If you can see cracks it is likely that the blade will fail if placed under pressure. As a general guide to standard blade width-to-thickness ratio, my supplier suggests the following values:

Blade width	Blade thickness
$\frac{1}{16}$in (1.5mm)	$\frac{25}{1000}$in (0.635mm)
$\frac{1}{8}$in (3mm)	$\frac{25}{1000}$in (0.635mm)
$\frac{1}{4}$in (6mm)	$\frac{25}{1000}$in (0.635mm)
$\frac{3}{8}$in (10mm)	$\frac{25}{1000}$in (0.635mm)
$\frac{1}{2}$in (12mm)	$\frac{25}{1000}$in (0.635mm)
$\frac{5}{8}$in (16mm)	$\frac{32}{1000}$in (0.813mm)
$\frac{3}{4}$in (19mm)	$\frac{32}{1000}$in (0.813mm)
1in (25mm)	$\frac{35}{1000}$in (0.889mm)

The above guide should be used when considering blades that will run over a bandsaw with two wheels. For those with three wheels most blades will be under 6ft (2m) long. In these instances a recommended thickness of $\frac{14}{1000}$in (0.356mm) is best up to $\frac{1}{2}$in (12mm) wide. It is probably unwise to try and use anything wider. This is far thinner than recommended for use on two-wheeled machines. It allows for more flexibility, but at some cost to life expectancy. Jointing this thickness of blade is difficult because there is not a great deal of material there to start with. If the manufacturer is not careful the joint will just waste away. Should you try to use thicker

Bandknife & Bandsaw by
DAKIN

Dakin Premier Saw Works, Sowerby Bridge HX6 2TN, UK

telephone order line 01422 831375
fax order line 01422 834589

B

information sheet

BANDKNIFE

K1
BANDKNIFE/SLITTING BLADE — Single Edge

CUTS
Textiles, Plastic foam, Latex
WIDTHS *(inches)*
3/8, 1/2, 5/8, 3/4, 1, 1 1/4, 1 1/2, 2
THICKNESS *(inches)*
.018, .020, .022, .024, .028

K2
BANDKNIFE BLADE — Double Edge

CUTS
Textiles, Plastic foam,
WIDTHS *(inches)*
1/4, 3/8, 1/2, 5/8, 3/4
THICKNESS
.016, .018, .020, .022
Also available twisted 180°

K3
BANDKNIFE BLADE — Single and Double Edge

CUTS
Plastic foam,
WIDTHS *(inches)*
3/8, 1/2, 5/8, 3/4
THICKNESS
.018, .020
Also available twisted 180°
TEETH
From 8tpi to 14tpi
40° Gullet, Equiangular

K4
BANDKNIFE BLADE — Single and Double Edge

CUTS
Plastic foam,
WIDTHS *(inches)*
3/8, 1/2, 5/8, 3/4, 1, 1 1/4
THICKNESS
.018, .020, .022, .024
TEETH
From 8tpi to 14tpi
40° Gullet, Equiangular

K5
BANDKNIFE BLADE — Single Edge

Used as perforating or saw blade
CUTS
Plastic foam,
WIDTHS *(inches)*
3/8 - 3
THICKNESS
.018 - .048
TEETH
From 8tpi to 14tpi
40° and 60° Gullet, Equiangular

K6
BANDKNIFE BLADE — Single Edge

Long Wave
WIDTHS *(inches)*
5/8, 3/4, 1
THICKNESS
.020, .024
PITCH
2 3/4" Wave

K7
BANDKNIFE BLADE — Single Edge

Short Wave
WIDTHS *(inches)*
1/2, 5/8, 3/4, 1
THICKNESS
.020, .024
PITCH
5/8", 3/4" and 1" Wave

K8
BANDKNIFE BLADE — Single Edge

Scalloped and Bevelled
WIDTHS *(inches)*
1/2, 5/8, 3/4, 1
THICKNESS
.020, .024
PITCH
3/8" and 1/2" Scallop

K9
BANDKNIFE BLADE — Single Edge

Angle Notched and Bevelled
WIDTHS *(inches)*
1/2, 5/8, 3/4, 1, 1 1/4
THICKNESS
.020, .024
PITCH
1/4", 3/8" and 1/2"

K10
BANDKNIFE BLADE — Single and Double Edge

Notched and Bevelled
CUTS
Tissue paper, Mineral wool fibre,
Insulation material,
Corrugated paper.
WIDTHS *(inches)*
5/8, 3/4, 1, 1 1/4
THICKNESS
.020, .024
PITCH
1/4", 3/8" and 1/2"

BANDSAW
FILE RESHARPENABLE

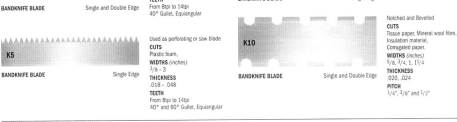

S1
BANDSAW BLADE — Single Edge

CUTS
Rigid Foam, Wood, Plastic
WIDTHS *(inches)*
1/4, 3/8, 1/2, 5/8, 3/4, 1, 1 1/4, 1 1/2, 2
THICKNESS
.018, .020, .024, .028
TEETH
2tpi – 10tpi

S2
BANDSAW BLADE — Double Edge

WIDTHS *(inches)*
1/4, 3/8, 1/2, 5/8, 3/4, 1, 1 1/4, 1 1/2, 2
THICKNESS
.018, .020, .024, .028, .032, .036, .040
TEETH
2tpi – 10tpi

S3
BANDSAW BLADE — Single and Double Edge

WIDTHS *(inches)*
3/8, 1/2, 5/8, 3/4, 1, 1 1/4, 1 1/2, 2
THICKNESS
.018, .020, .024, .028
TEETH
Offset or Not Offset. Equiangular

SPECIALS *prices on request*

X1
TEXTILE TENTERING BAND — Single Edge

Needle point
WIDTHS *(inches)*
3/4, 1
THICKNESS
.020, .028
PITCH
1/4" point to point

X2
IONISING STRIP

WIDTH *(inches)* 1/8
THICKNESS .004
TEETH 55tpi

X3
CONTOUR BLADE

Friction wire - 14 core
DIAMETER *(inches)* .023

EDGES		
SB/SE	Single Bevel – Single Edge
DB/SE	Double Bevel – Single Edge
SB/DE	Single Bevel – Double Edge
DB/DE	Double Bevel – Double Edge

Fig 58 A whole host of small bandsaw blades, for a multitude of uses!
(Reproduced with the permission of Dakin & Co. (Saws) Ltd.)

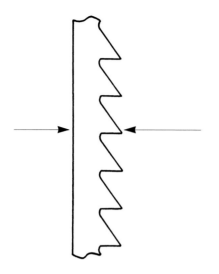

Fig 59 Points from which to measure the 'width' of a bandsaw blade.

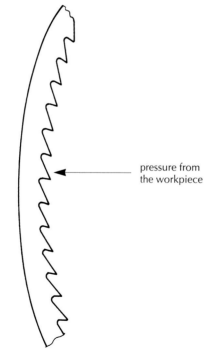

pressure from
the workpiece

Fig 60 Exaggeration of a narrow blade deflecting backwards away from the workpiece as it is fed through the machine.

blades on three-wheeled machines, they will surely fail through fatigue. Flexibility must be right for the size of wheels on your bandsaw. If in any doubt, refer to the manufacturer or your blade supplier.

The width of the blade used on your bandsaw should also be appropriate for the type of cutting you wish to undertake. The number of teeth per inch and their shape will also have some bearing on this, but we will come to that later. If you wish to produce straight cuts, say working off a fence, common sense should indicate that you do not use your narrowest blade.

Small blades under ³⁄₁₆in (5mm) in width are designed to cut curved work and will not withstand continuous maintained pressure over long periods. Medium-range blades up to ³⁄₈in (10mm) flex less than the very narrow blades, but again are not really suitable for continuous rip sawing. Therefore it follows that for general purposes a large ½in (12mm) or wider blade is probably the most efficient and useful. I keep one on the machine most of the time.

In conjunction with blade width we must also take into consideration the sharpness of the blade, wheel alignment, guide set-up, type of teeth and feed speed (how fast you push the material through the machine). Some of these we have already discussed in the previous chapters and others we will be covering later. Any single factor or a combination of them may cause your blade to deflect or wander in the cut. Smaller blades will tend to deflect backwards, away from the cutting edge, because they do not have the body strength to resist pressure. The larger blades, because they are stronger, may tend to deflect off to one side or another. If the cut wanders in any way, first check that the machine is set up correctly. Has the correct tension been applied? Is the blade tracked and are the guides set correctly? Determine if the teeth are dull. Very hard wood, pieces with interlocked grain and included defects can also cause the blade to wander during use.

The width of the blade also has a critical effect in relation to the arc of any radius you may wish to cut. The determining factors will be the width of blade and the set of the teeth. Blades will not cut a tight radius if the back edge and one side of the blade are rubbing in the cavity and effectively filling the space created by the saw cut.

Relief cuts can be made to convex and concave curves to allow the use of larger blades, but the finished surface quality will not be as good. We will cover this area in a later chapter. Widening the 'set' on a blade will also allow the cutting radius to be reduced. This can only be achieved on silver steel blades, but it is a questionable practice, increasing the amount of waste from the cut. Another possibility for tightening the cutting radii is rounding the back edge of the blade with a file, but frankly I believe little is gained. Some maintain that this should be practised when small, narrower blades keep on breaking, but I believe that if the cause of the breakages was analysed, in all likelihood a fault in the set-up of the machine would be found. The best way to cut tight curves and shapes is to use the correct blade for the job. The following table gives an indication of the tightest cutting radius for each of the blade widths, assuming standard setting:

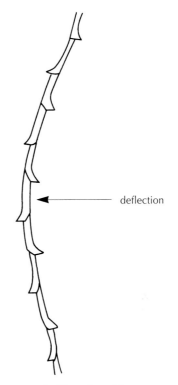

Fig 61 *Exaggerated effect of a wider blade deflecting to one side of the cut.*

Blade width	Minimum cutting radius
¹⁄₁₆in (1.5mm)	Should cut at 90 degrees.
⅛in (3mm)	¼in radii (6mm)
³⁄₁₆in (5mm)	⁵⁄₁₆in (8mm)
¼in (6mm)	⅜in (10mm)
⅜in (10mm)	1½in (38mm)
½in (12mm)	2½in (64mm)
⅝in (16mm)	4in (100mm)
¾in (19mm)	5½in (140mm)
1in (25mm)	7in (180mm)

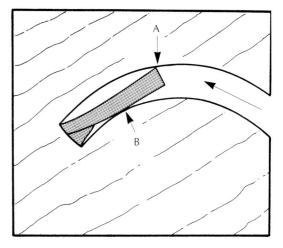

Fig 62 *A small bandsaw blade cutting an arc. The restrictions are at points A and B, where the blade's side and back rub against the sides of the cavity cut by the teeth.*

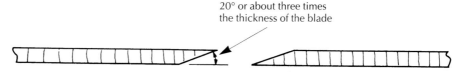

20° or about three times
the thickness of the blade

Fig 63 Exaggerated view of joint prior to brazing and the correct angles.

JOINTING BLADES

Silver steel blades can be jointed, re-jointed and sharpened fairly easily without high-tech equipment. The softer steel used in their manufacture facilitates this. Some users swear by them, claiming it to be far more economical to buy a coil of pre-shaped steel and cut off lengths as and when required. Broken blades can be re-jointed, but care should be exercised. Establishing the cause of the break initially is important – if the blade has broken once, it may well do so again. Kits for brazing these blades are readily available and are reasonably inexpensive. If you wish to

Fig 64 Blank bandsaw blade ends filed to the correct angles.

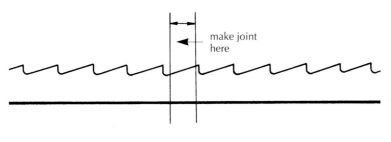

make joint
here

Fig 65 The most appropriate area in which to joint a blade.

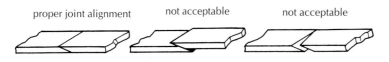

proper joint alignment   not acceptable   not acceptable

Fig 66 Correct alignment is essential to the process of forming a sound joint.

Fig 67 Here the blade is set up in a holder. Flux has been applied and the strip of solder can clearly be seen positioned over the joint.

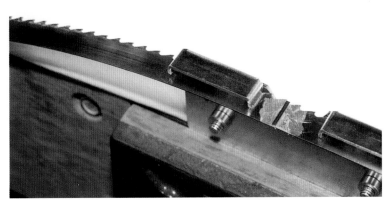

Fig 68 Here the blade is shown after jointing but prior to cleaning up. My first attempts were far from perfect, but even this joint, with rather a large amount of braze left on the surface, managed to weld.

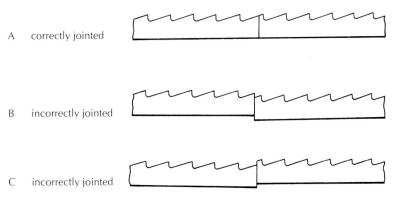

A   correctly jointed

B   incorrectly jointed

C   incorrectly jointed

Fig 69 Diagram A shows the back of the blade correctly aligned. If your joint is made like B or C, it will cause problems.

have a go, and have some silver steel saw blade material, ask your existing saw blade supplier for a kit. The process is not too difficult but needs practice to achieve a joint that will last.

Having determined the overall length of the blade, each end to be jointed should be filed on opposing faces at 20 degrees.

A kit that I tested for this book was supplied by 'BriMarc' and made in the US. It has a holder that retains the ends of the blades at the correct angle for grinding. Try to cut the blank so that the joint falls slightly behind the tooth face. This helps to take some of the strain away from the leading edge, and hopefully should prolong the life of the joint.

Having filed or ground the joint to a satisfactory fit the blade ends are placed in the holder supplied. With spring set teeth you may have to flatten the set slightly to ensure the two faces meet snugly. After the blade is jointed, the teeth can be re-set. The holder will maintain the position of the blade during the brazing process. The braze is usually supplied in strip or wire form and uses a flux that prevents the metal from oxidizing during the intense heat of the brazing process. When the blade is correctly positioned, heat is applied, following the manufacturer's process instructions, until the joint is made.

Afterwards, clean off any excess braze. Check that the joint is sound by gently flexing it over a 10–12in (250–300mm) radius. If you have a three-pulley machine it is likely that a smaller radius should be used for testing. Be careful lining up the blade when jointing. One that is slightly out of line will damage the thrust-bearings and will be very difficult to keep on track and on the wheels!

Although it might be worth considering jointing your own blades, many of us cannot afford the time to do this. If, like me, you tend to use the flexi backed blades for most uses, you will not be able to achieve a really successful joint by brazing. Industrial and professional jointers tend to use 'butt'

Fig 70 Marty initially selects the correct blank blade specification for the order he is going to make up. Notice under the bench there is a whole row of boxed blank coils and the resistance welder is in the background.

or 'resistance welders'. To find out more about how this jointing is carried out I visited my supplier in Tewkesbury, following through the sequence of events.

The companies who make up the saw blades from blanks are supplied by the manufacturer with coils pre-packed in wooden or plastic boxes to avoid damage to the teeth. The first job is to select the right blade coil depending upon width, gauge, type of tooth, tpi, etc. Having selected the appropriate coil the blank is measured out on the bench against a fixed tape.

In this case the blank is cut to length using a radial arm cross-cut saw fitted with a metal cutting disc. The next job is to set the resistance welder to the appropriate settings for the gauge of saw to be jointed. The duration of the welding process is critical – too long and the joint will burn out, too short and it will fail.

Before putting the blank into the welder the rough ends need to be filed smooth. In addition to this any detritus or waste needs cleaning from the welder jaws. Foreign bodies such as loose bits of metal will affect the overall performance of the joint. The blank is set up in the welder, looping it over the top. The two ends to be jointed are brought together and clamped in place. During the welding process they are forced together by a predetermined amount to make the joint.

The welder applies enough heat to the joint to fuse the two ends together. After the welding process is completed, in a matter of seconds, the joint is left to cool off before removal.

The ridges created by fusing the blade together need to be ground off flat on the faces. There is also a ridge on the back edge of the blade that needs to be removed. This is easily done while the blade is held in the annealer. During welding the joint is 'air'-hardened and becomes very brittle. Annealing is the process that restores the correct hardness and strength to the blade by re-heating the joint and cooling it slowly.

Prior to annealing the joint looks bright and shiny because it has been cleaned up. Applying the heat during the annealing process 'blues' the jointed area. This annealing of the joint is as important as the weld itself; unless it is done properly, the blade will surely break!

After the blade has cooled down the operator visually checks the joint for quality. This is something that you should always do yourself when purchasing new

Fig 71 With the blank laid out it is cut to length using a radial arm cross-cut saw fitted with a metal-cutting disc.

Fig 72 The blank is set into the welder, coiled at the top, and the jaws adjusted.

Fig 73 Here you can see the weld being formed. The operator looks away during this process to avoid eye damage.

Fig 74 In the welding machine, the joint can be seen as a ridge where the melted ends have been fused together.

Fig 75 The joint cleaned up and set prior to annealing.

Fig 76 The annealing process in action – note the changed colour of the blade.

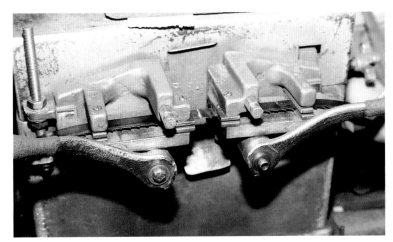

Fig 77 The final test is to bend the blade around a smaller radius than the wheels on the bandsaw upon which it will be used.

blades. The final test for the joint is to gently bend it round a fairly small radius The radius should be less than the size of bandsaw wheel the blade is likely to be put round in use. Narrower, thinner blades should bend more easily round a small curve; thicker, wider ones round a larger curve.

Butt welding of blades like this for the wood-cutting industry is done off the machine. Some sophisticated equipment in the metal-cutting industry has a welder on one side of the machine. This allows for blades to be jointed when cutting internal holes in a workpiece. The blade is passed through a hole bored in the workpiece at an appropriate position, then jointed. The cutting process takes place and the joint is broken to remove the workpiece. Fortunately there are easier ways for us to cut holes in wood than this!

MAINTENANCE

Looking after your blades is important: dull, kinked, clogged and rusty blades will not perform as efficiently as they should. Common sense must prevail – do not let the cutting edges come into contact with metal or concrete. If you have to place them on the ground, make sure the teeth are face upwards. If a fine-pitched blade has become clogged, take it off the machine, fold it up and leave it to soak in a cleaning solution, diesel is fine for this. Once softened clean off with a fine wire brush working away from the cutting edge.

It is a good idea to oil any blades you do not have currently in use. Also lightly oil the blades before you put them on the saw.

It is a foregone conclusion that your blade will eventually break, but most blades fail because they have been misused.

Over-tensioning will stretch and stress the blade, under-tensioning will allow it to wander and twist away from the cutting edge. Guides and thrust-bearings that have been set too closely, or loosely, will cause problems. A machine that is too lightweight or which vibrates too much will shorten blade life. Careless operators who force work through the machine or who fail to ensure all the setting-up factors are right will probably have the most detrimental effect on blades.

SETTING AND SHARPENING

If you are using silver steel blades they will eventually need to be sharpened and reset to maintain clean accurate cutting. Always set the blade first, followed by sharpening. In order to cut correctly, spring set bandsaw blades must be set by bending alternate teeth out of line to either side of the body. This creates the cutting width, or kerf, of the blade. Hand setting is carried out by a pliers-type tool that can be adjusted to increase or decrease the amount of set. This set is normally around 25 per cent of the body thickness. Mark the blade with chalk at the start and work your way around alternately until the mark is reached. It cannot be guaranteed that hand setting will leave all teeth cutting, but hopefully only one or two will miss. One way to establish how successful the setting has been can be employed. Put the blade onto the machine and tension and track as usual. Bring forward the back thrust-bearings temporarily and run up the machine. Using a fine grit stone, apply it carefully to both sides of the blade until it just touches. Be sure to wear goggles and keep your hands away from the blade. When you subsequently sharpen the blade you should clearly see that some of the teeth have not been touched by the stone.

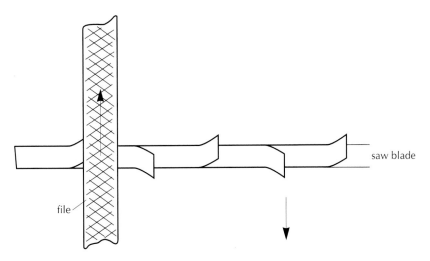

file

saw blade

*Fig 78 The direction in which the file is used
when sharpening a spring set bandsaw blade.*

These teeth can be lightly sharpened,
those that have been touched should be
sharpened normally until the flat caused
by the stone has disappeared.

To sharpen the blade by hand with a
three-corner file you need to be able to
hold it firmly at the point at which you are
working. Support the blade either side
with a strip of wood or ply and place in the
vice. Make sure you are working at a comfortable angle (sitting down if necessary),
mark the blade with chalk where you start.
The file should be presented to the tooth
face at 90 degrees.

Work on alternate teeth, filing toward
the outside cutting edge. This will leave
any burrs behind that edge where they will
not impede performance or waste
removal. Continue in this fashion until the
blade is finished. Remember it is unlikely
that you will be able to sharpen any blade
with hardened tips – these will have to be
mechanically ground. At the end of the
day you will have to weigh up the cost of
your supplier regrinding the blades, if he
has the facilities to do so, against a
straightforward replacement.

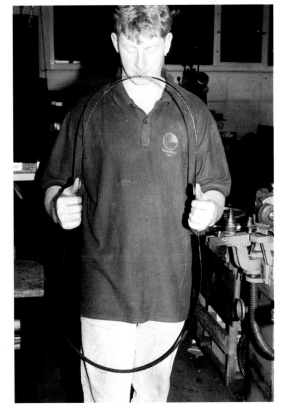

*Fig 79 The first stage in folding a
bandsaw for storage. Grasp the blade
firmly, thumbs behind, bottom loop
resting on your thigh.*

59

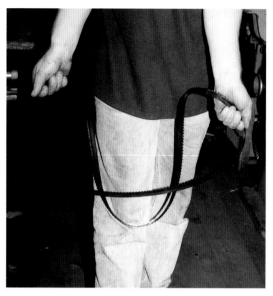

*Fig 80 In stage two, move your hands
down and turn your wrists out.*

STORAGE

The easiest way to store blades when not in
use is to fold them up into three loops.
There are various ways in which to do this,
but the experts say the following way is
best. First, hold the blade firmly, teeth
away from you, resting the bottom edge on
your thigh. With your thumbs behind the
blade, gently force the blade down, turning your wrists out at the same time.

Bring your hands together and the
loops will begin to form. To hold them in
place tie with string or lightweight wire.

I have been kindly supplied with a fault
finding chart for bandsaw blades by one of
the UK manufacturers, this is to be found
under Appendix 2.

Fig 81 Bring your hands across each other in stage three.

four

FIRST CUTS

HAND POSITIONS

Safety procedures are addressed in the final chapter. What must be remembered is that the blades used on the machine are metal, and your fingers are flesh and blood. They do not mix together well. Having said that, the bandsaw is probably one of the safer sawing machines to operate, complacency aside. The blade action forces the workpiece down onto the table of the machine, not back at the operator as circular saws do. The cutting edge is at the front and can be guarded successfully except on rare occasions. You should always use a push-stick in preference to

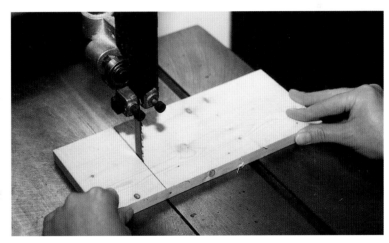

Fig 82 Straight-line cutting. Hold the workpiece firmly at each corner and proceed with the cutting action. The required component piece is to the left of the saw blade; cut to the right-hand side of the line.

Fig 83 Cross-cutting small components from a workpiece using the fence and a push stick.

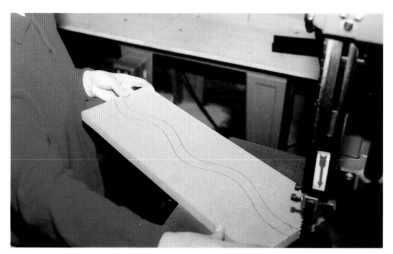

Fig 84 Presenting a workpiece lined up with the blade when cutting curves.

fingers. In the unfortunate event of a breakage or the blade coming off, movement ceases just about immediately. It might sound horrendous, but not too much damage will be done except to the blade. Switch off quickly and work out why it happened, if you do not already know. Most of the photographs in this book will show the top guide assembly pulled up out of the way – this is for clarity; please remember this.

With the machine set, blades tensioned and tracked correctly, it is now down to the operator to develop his technique. The ideal is to present your workpiece to the cutting edge with a smooth and continuous feed. This should assure a quality of surface finish that will be acceptable. To achieve this you must think through your hand positions before you start cutting. Always hold the workpiece firmly, but not in such a way that you feel rigid and jerky when cutting. For simple straight-line cutting, mark your project and hold the piece firmly at each corner. Proceed to present it to the cutting edge and push smoothly through. If perhaps you hear the motor slow down at any point, you are probably exerting too much pressure. Ease off the cutting action until you 'feel' the bandsaw

is cutting within its capabilities. It is unlikely that this will happen often, unless you are cutting something particularly hard or are being over-enthusiastic with the feed rate of the workpiece.

If cross-cutting several short-length items, use a fence and push stick. Grasp the workpiece firmly with the right hand, holding it against the fence with sufficient pressure to maintain that position during the cut. With the left hand holding the push-stick, push the workpiece through the machine. This is a useful technique for cutting lots of short lengths, and keeps your fingers away from the blade.

Cutting curves requires a little more thought and dexterity. When presenting the workpiece to the cutting edge it has to be positioned in such a way that the leading edge lines up with the blade. The right hand will lead. The left follows, controlling the movement to right or left to create the curve. Very often, depending upon the acuteness of the curves, it may be necessary to switch hands as the workpiece swings from one side to the other as the cut is made. As time goes on you will develop your own techniques for dealing with this type of cut. Whatever happens, it is best to ensure you feel comfortable as the cutting action proceeds; otherwise the result will be a jerky, unevenly finished surface. If you have to change hand positions during the cut, just ease the workpiece back towards you slightly to ensure that the blade runs free. Switch over and then you can lead back into the cut with the new hand position.

On occasions it may be necessary to bring one or other set of fingers into close proximity with the blade. When this happens, you may be cutting a small bit of waste from a component; just take care and be totally relaxed about what is happening. If your actions are stilted or stiff you may fail to fully control the workpiece. The hand away from the cutting edge must do most of the work, with the other just there for guidance.

Hand positions are important. With some longer and wider workpieces it is necessary to plan your route of approach and exit. It may be that the component is turned around and cutting starts again from the other end. Be careful if you try to back out of the first cut – you may pull the blade off when bringing the workpiece back towards you. If this is likely to happen, turn off before you attempt to remove it.

Smoothness of operation and rotation of workpieces comes with practice. Just remember the basics and it will not take long for you to develop your skill.

THE RIGHT BLADE

We have already discussed at length the differing types of blade and how they are made up. It is important, when setting out to start cutting, that the appropriate blade is selected for the job in hand. Many times a universal blade can be left on the machine and will not need to be changed unless a specific job is being undertaken. Most users will settle on probably half a

dozen or so differing types and sizes of blade. These will accommodate the general range of circumstances likely to be encountered. This is not an ideal situation, but is economically sensible. If a specific job requires a special blade it is better to buy in at that point, rather than keep one 'on the shelf' just in case. This general approach starts to fall down when you have run out of larger blades and need to cut some thick stuff and only have a small blade available. Misusing blades is the quickest way to reduce their cutting efficiency, blunt and break them. Try to think and plan ahead for each cutting project.

Most blades will drop into the following categories:

	Small	Medium	Large
Width:			
(imperial)	1/16 – 1/8in	3/16 – 3/8in	1/2in plus
(metric)	1.5–3.0mm	5–9mm	12mm plus
Pitch:	14–32tpi	4–12tpi	2–4tpi

For general purpose use I tend to keep a 1/2in (12mm) flexi-backed blade with 4 tpi on the machine at most times, changing this as and when I need. This is all right for most straight cuts and a few gentle curves. If the curves and radiuses become more acute or very tight, I use a medium or small blade. The width of the blade will determine the curve you can cut smoothly in your workpiece. As a reminder, refer to the table in Chapter 3 giving the blade width to radius ratios.

When cutting curves it is a good idea to try a test piece first, to see if the blade you have selected will actually cut as you want. Remember a smaller blade will cut a tighter curve than a larger one. Use a smaller one in preference to forcing the larger one round the curves. There are some techniques to overcome this under certain circumstances that we will discuss

Fig 85 A ⅜in (10mm) flexi-backed blade cutting gentle curves. Note the blade cuts to the right of the pencil line at all times and does not cross over.

Fig 86 Burn or rub marks clearly seen on the cut curved surface. The blade used was far too wide for the radius cut.

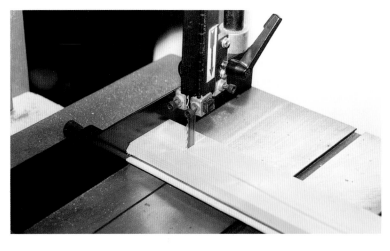

Fig 87 Cross-cutting to length using the fence assembly. The piece nearest the fence is the component required; repeat cuts will make more of these if need be.

Fig 88 'Ripping' a workpiece to width.

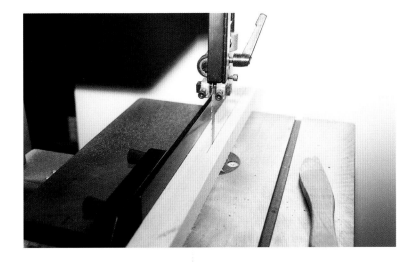

Fig 89 'Deep' cutting a workpiece.

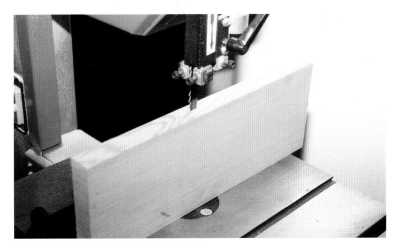

Fig 90 The workpiece taken off the saw to illustrate the pinching action.

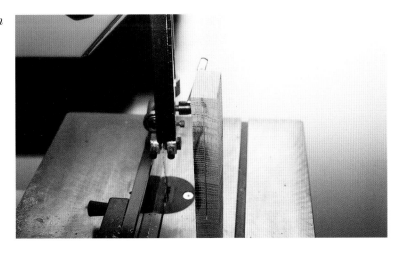

later in the chapter. To run your test piece, mark some scrap with the appropriate curves and proceed to cut on the bandsaw. Decide which side will be the component and which will be the waste, and cut to the waste side of the line. Carry through the cut until complete.

You will discover very quickly if the blade you have fitted is too large, when you will not be able to cut round the first curve. If this happens, do not try to remove the workpiece while the machine is running. Switch off and wait till the blade has stopped moving. Proceed by changing the blade for a smaller one and try again. If the curves have been cut, but you felt the blade 'binding' as the workpiece went through, it is most likely that the back edge of the blade has been rubbing in the cut. Tell-tale signs of this can be seen when the workpiece is split open after cutting. The black marks are caused by the back edge rubbing and burning the workpiece. It is obvious in these cases that the blade is too large to cut the curves required; change to a smaller one.

Apart from cutting curves, the small bandsaw has a host of other basic uses. Cross-cutting – cutting across the width of the grain, can be achieved free hand, working to a pencil line. Alternatively, make the cuts using the fence for those repetitive jobs. In both cases choose a larger blade for this operation and, depending upon the finished cut surface required, use a standard or skip-tooth blade. The speed at which you feed the material through the machine helps determine the quality of surface finish. Rushing it through just because the machine's motor will stand it is not always the best policy.

'Rip' sawing or 'ripping' stock is described as cutting along the length of the grain, but applies when cutting through the thinner dimension. 'Deep' cutting, which also cuts along the length of the grain, is when the workpiece is being cut on its edge through the thicker dimension.

When rip cutting, the feed speed can be much greater than when deeping. If you try to force a workpiece through when deeping, the blade will clog. It will overheat and invariably break, wander off course or burn the stock. Try to keep the feed speed constant, helping to ensure an even cut throughout. Slight pauses will result in some surface unevenness; unfortunately, they are sometimes difficult to avoid when deep cutting.

Ripping along the grain can be a useful technique for producing thin strips of wood for veneering or inlay work. In these cases use the table fence to set the width of cut, but it will be the 'falling' piece that becomes your component for use. Normally you have to cut this way round. The guide assembly needs to be set right down on your work – it becomes difficult if the table fence is in the way. You will also be able to see clearly how the blade is performing in the cut. Make sure it is sharp, or it might break out of the side of the workpiece, rendering useless the thin component.

For various projects you may need to make diagonal cuts across the angle of the grain. Individual cuts can be made freehand, but if a large number of repeat work needs to be carried out, it is useful to use a jig. The next chapter will cover this area in more detail.

Cutting 'with the grain' can be required on occasions. The grain in this case runs from the top to the bottom of the cut.

It is possible that you may come across problems with the workpiece binding or pinching on the blade as the cut is made. We will not go into too much detail here as to why that may happen, except to say that the wood is most likely 'case hardened'. It is probable that the outer skin has shrunk more than the inner during drying. If this does occur it is best to stop the cutting action and fit a small wedge into the cut. This forces the two parts wider to give the necessary clearance to the blade. Using wedges is a perfectly acceptable practice and helps overcome the problem of binding. This occurs most often with hardwoods that have been dried too quickly or incorrectly. When you have the wedge in place, start the machine and recommence sawing.

CUTTING SEQUENCES

I use a lot of templates, especially when I am likely to be making the same component some time in the future. My range covers everything from rocking horse components, table ends, to legs and axe handles. As a point of interest I find it very useful to write critical dimensions and comments on the templates to help me with production at some later date. To sort out cutting sequences the next section uses a couple of templates and photographs to take us through the routines.

We will start by looking at the front of the model train. Mark around the template continuously and clearly on the outer edges. Initially start by cutting a relief cut into the point at which the arcs meet, at the bottom of the workpiece. Cut also along the two straight lines to each side.

Both these sets of relief cuts will allow the blade to come free from the workpiece when it reaches the sharp corners. Even with a very small blade it is pointless trying to turn in such a small space. The blade fitted to the machine at this time is too large to cut continuously around the outline. To achieve the objective of cutting round the curve we will need to take one of two actions.

The first way to overcome this situation is to cut a whole series of relief cuts at fairly regular intervals around the outer curve. This releases the blade, allowing the curve to be formed. The cutting sequence in this case starts by leading in at

the top on a line that will meet the outer curve of the component. As the cutting edge of the blade hits the relief cuts continuous progress can be made. Follow right round until the cut meets the original relief cut in the sharp corner.

There is an alternative to cutting lots of relief cuts. This uses the cutting edge of the blade to create a wide enough space around it to allow free movement. The lead into the second cut in this case flows from the side already cut. Follow the outer curve, cutting as you go. Very soon the blade will be in a position where, to go any further, it will have to be forced – don't. Back up slightly and widen the width of cut by 'nibbling' away at the waste side. This will have to be done regularly as you make progress around the outer curve. A pattern will appear with the widening taking place at every blade–width of cut. Eventually you will achieve your objective and meet the relief cut in the sharp corner. Using both nibbling and relief cutting methods is time-consuming – it is better to cut with a small blade that easily accommodates the radius. Of course there are times when the quality of finished surface, etc., is not critical, and it is a useful technique to learn.

Cutting a series of straightforward outer curves is fairly simple. When faced with a set of curves that flow from opposing directions, however, things get more complicated. The next combinations discussed use similar techniques but to produce flowing convex and concave curves. The objective in this case is to cut a front valance for a small book-case using a template that is reversed to produce the required outline. In the first instance relief cuts are made into the sharp corners adjacent to the sweeping curves in the middle. The first outline cut leads in from one side and follows the outer line until it hits the first relief cut.

The workpiece is reversed and the second cut follows on from the first

Fig 91 A wedge in place, forcing the cut out to allow clearance for the blade to cut. Put the wedge in place when the workpiece is back in the cutting position.

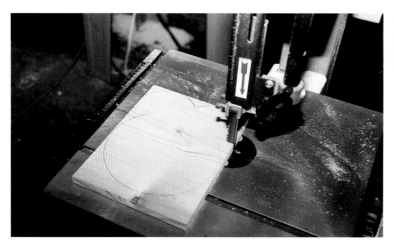

Fig 92 Relief cuts made into the point at which the arcs meet at the bottom and along the straight edges.

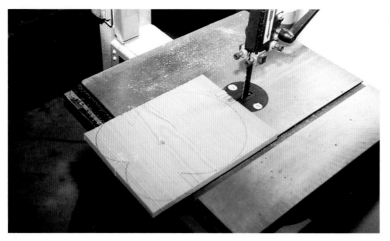

Fig 93 Relief cuts made around one side of the component prior to cutting the outer curve.

Fig 94 Continuous cutting is maintained until the blade reaches the original relief cut into the corner.

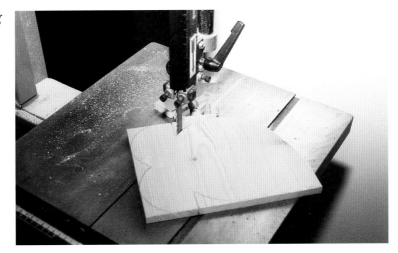

Fig 95 To cut the other outer curve, lead in from the cut side onto the line. In this case no relief cuts have been made.

Fig 96 The blade has been 'backed' up and the cut 'nibbled' away to allow free movement of the blade around the outer curve.

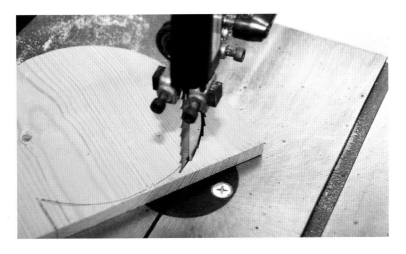

Fig 97 The first profile cut leads into the sweeping curve and hits the relief cut.

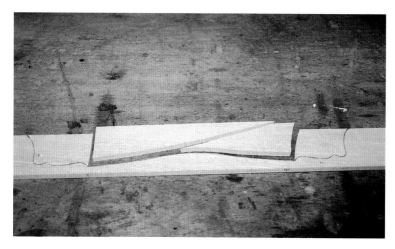

Fig 98 The second cut leads up from the first around the curve and into the relief cut.

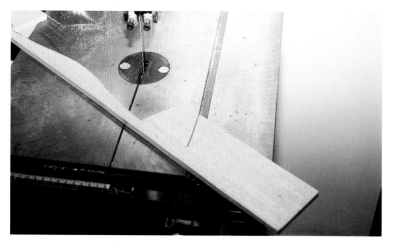

Fig 99 A relief cut into the bottom of the easiest corner.

around the outline and into the relief cut. On the one end we will nibble our way round. Start with a relief into the bottom of the easiest curve. Nibble your way round as previously described working down into the relief cut.

Approach from the other side into the curves, nibbling your way round again. The final cutting on this side is an outer curve that can easily be trimmed off.

On the other side, a mass of relief cuts has been made as the alternative method of cutting. Either of these methods can be applied to this type of profile-cutting and depends upon whichever you feel happy with. The outcome is the same but the waste on one side is a lot smaller in size than the other.

Another technique used to create relief points when cutting is to drill out rounded corners before work commences.

Adopting this process will again allow a larger blade to be used. It also makes the job that much easier because most of the cuts will be straight lines or gentle curves. Naturally if you are about to commence cutting a series of tight curves it is better to have a smaller blade fitted to obviate the need for relief cutting. With most jobs you will find there is a fair chance that what-

Fig 100 'Nibbling' your way round; cut down and round the curve to the relief.

Fig 101 The cut above the current one has already been made and another partly nibbled back into the second small curve to meet the oncoming cut.

Fig 102 Finally trim off the last outer curves. Note the pencil line is still visible on the workpiece.

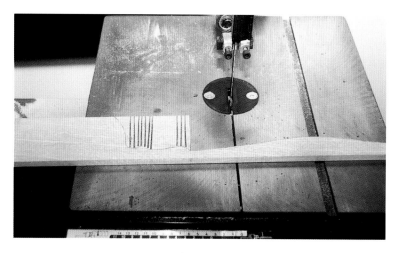

Fig 103 Lots of relief cuts around the 'tight' curves.

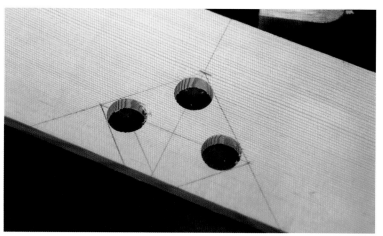

Fig 104 Another method of relief using pre-drilled holes. For one-offs it may be quicker to drill out the corners and cut the straight lines with a bandsaw if you have a blade fitted that will not cut the radius – this avoids having to keep changing the blade.

Fig 105 The job completed, ready for cleaning up.

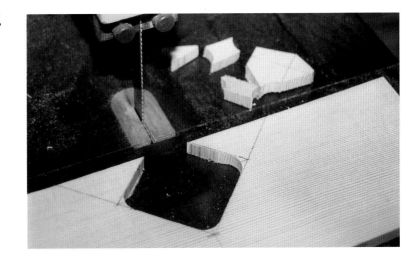

Fig 106 Using a turning hole to cut sharp points. Once past the point, turn the blade, cutting all the while, in as tight a circle as possible before returning to the cutting line.

Fig 107 The turning hole technique allows sharp corners and points to be cut without the blade leaving the workpiece.

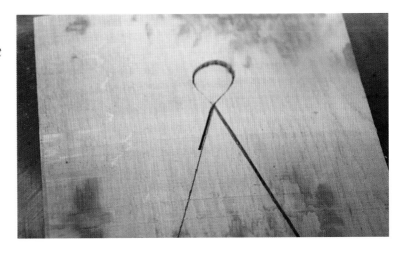

ever size blade is used, some relief work will be necessary.

At another extreme you may find the need to cut sharp points or corners without withdrawing the saw blade from the work-piece. To achieve this you will need to employ a technique known as 'turning holes'. This basically involves following usual cutting practice along the approach side to the point. Then, when you have gone past the point or corner, turning the blade round in a tightly cut circle before returning to the correct track to cut the finished profile. This is a useful technique when using a very small blade on an intricate profile without much room to manoeuvre.

Following the above guidelines will allow the user to become familiar with his machine and gain confidence to tackle most jobs. Experience is worth a great deal and as time goes on, individual techniques will develop to allow better control and quality of work.

CHAPTER

ADVANCING YOUR SKILLS

Most small bandsaws are fitted with a variety of attachments that can be very useful for cutting straight, at angles and circular work. Some machines like my old one do not have any of these fancy bits, and that is when innovation must take over.

TILTING BEDS

I guess the majority of machines, even the most basic, will have a work table that tilts. This will allow you to produce straight angle cuts along the length of a workpiece. If you are one of the unfortunates who does not have this facility, look out in the next chapter for the simple jig that will enable you to do this. Assuming at this point that you are able to tilt the saw table, you will find somewhere on the machine a calibrated scale. This allows for the angle of cut to be set when the locking nuts or levers have been released.

It is always a good idea to calibrate the settings before you start, by checking to see if the 90 degree angle is being cut correctly first. Set the marker to zero and with luck you should find that the tilted angle set from the scale is close or spot on to the required one. Always check anyway by cutting a bit of waste stock. Be sure when you tilt the table that there is enough clearance around the throat insert to allow the whole thing to move freely without applying pressure on the blade. Most tables with plastic inserts are cut wide enough to allow for this. On the older machines or those with replaceable wooden inserts they may have to be made larger to begin with. I tend to

keep an old wider insert handy for this and just swap them round when required.

The table fence needs to be set at the bottom of the slope away from the blade. This enables the workpiece to be fed through the machine safely because it is supported against it. If you are unable to do this make a false fence to provide support for the workpiece. Trying to hold a component up against a fence on the top side is not satisfactory. It will possibly provide a distraction from the cutting action that may then lead to problems. With the fence set at the correct measured distance from the blade, feed the workpiece through the machine at a steady pace. Any width of blade can be used for this type of work, but I would always recommend the use of a larger one when performing straight-cut operations. Providing these simple instructions are observed, single- or multiple-angle cuts with the grain can be produced with ease.

MITRE GAUGES

A sliding mitre gauge is a very useful piece of kit, if supplied with your machine. Not only will it allow you to cut a variety of angles across the grain, it can also be used as an attachment for repetitive cross-cutting. Mitre gauges are generally fitted with a sliding scale marked with degrees. They should be calibrated to zero, right angle to the blade, before work starts.

These gauges tend to run in a T-shaped channel cut into the saw table. This should have been machined in line with the saw

Fig 108 *A tilting table arrangement showing the table tilted at 20 degrees on the sliding scale. These should be calibrated before use. Always use a bit of waste wood to check that the angle is cut to the desired degree.*

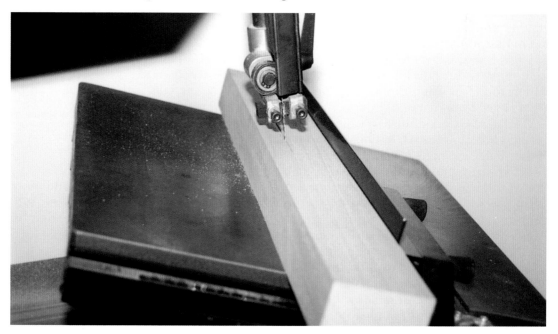

Fig 109 *A workpiece being cut on a tilted table. Note the fence giving support on the lower side.*

Fig 110 *This is a detail of the sliding scale on a typical mitre gauge. Do not forget to calibrate it and ensure that it cuts the angles indicated.*

Fig 111 *The sliding mitre gauge can also be used to cross-cut at right angles. In this instance a stop has been attached to the table to ensure each piece is cut to exactly the same length.*

cut in the factory, but sometimes things do not quite work out, hence the need to calibrate. Use a piece of waste wood to check the desired angle is being cut. For repetitive work, some machines are fitted with a length stop. These are useful, but really should be confined to use with shorter lengths of timber; longer ones will tend to become unwieldy and uncontrollable.

If you have a lot of short lengths that need cross-cutting to the same size, use the sliding mitre gauge attachment for this. A simple way to set the length is to fix a stop on the opposite side to the slide against which you set your workpiece before passing through the saw cut. Alternatively, use the table fence in a similar fashion. If you only wish to cut partly through use a depth stop in a similar way. Set the workpiece against the length stop and proceed with the cut until the workpiece reaches the depth stop. This technique can usefully be adapted for cutting shoulders on tenons.

SINGLE-POINT CUTTING

In addition to using the standard table fence, there is an interesting technique called 'single-point' cutting. This has the added benefit of being able to compensate for those blades that have a 'leading' cut to one side or another. Simply take a piece of waste wood, preferably something hard, say 1in (25mm) thick by 1½in (38mm) wide and round the one end. The piece should be long enough to be cramped to the saw table with a G-cramp or similar. Set at a slight angle to the blade on the left or right-hand side. This depends upon which is most comfortable for you, and the width of the workpiece. The rounded point should be leading slightly ahead of the cutting edge of the saw blade. This will enable the workpiece to make contact with the support before the cut commences. Measure your width of cut from the outer edge

of the saw kerf nearest the single-point support to its crown. This is not an exact science, and test pieces should be run if measurements are critical.

The workpiece should be presented to the cutting edge just after it has made contact with the crown of the single-point support. If your blade has demonstrated a desire to 'lead' to one side or the other, you are now able to compensate for that by adjusting the angle of approach made by the workpiece. Feed the component through the saw cut, keeping light pressure upon the single-point crown. Using this technique you are able to produce any number of equal widths ripped off a workpiece.

One variation of single-point cutting can be adopted for wider deep cutting. This helps to provide support along most of the width of the workpiece. You do this by making a support that can be clamped to the saw table. It is therefore thin at one end while the other end is flared up to provide a right-angle edge from which the workpiece can be guided. Similar to rip sawing using this technique, any slight lead on the blade's behalf can be compensated for. Take note, if you are trying to produce quality work while deep cutting with a suspect blade, you will probably fail. The workpiece needs to be in contact with the high support just prior to the sawing action commencing. Light pressure should be applied to keep it in place during the cutting action. This technique can be particularly useful when you are trying to cut thin slivers off some stock to make a veneer.

CUTTING CURVES

Single-point cutting techniques can be used to cut curves also, but first we will look at using the table fence for this. Remember that the radius of cut is directly related to the width of blade – look at the chart in Chapter 4. For most gentle curve works a ⅛in (12mm) or ⅜in (10mm) blade will do. Let's assume you wish to edge a round table made in, say, veneer-faced ply. If you feel unable to bend and laminate thin strips around the circumference, you may wish to just lay and glue on ready curved and cut pieces. First simply work out the arc that you wish to produce, mark this onto a piece of suitable stock and cut carefully around it freehand.

The next stage is to set your fence at a suitable distance from the cutting edge of the blade to produce the lipping to be laminated to the edge. Always add a bit to allow for cleaning up. Present the curved workpiece to the cutting edge, making contact with the fence just prior to the cutting action commencing. The workpiece will be angled away from the fence and the trailing edge should be brought round to follow through as the cut proceeds. Any number of curved strips can be produced in this way. They can be varied in thickness to suit their application. Allowance should be made to trim the ends off the finished pieces because, if you are like me, it's unlikely that they will all be perfect.

Another simple way to cut repeat curves is to use the waste offcut as the fence or guide in the cutting action. As before, mark out an arc on your workpiece and cut carefully around it to produce a clean smooth finish. The offcut is then clamped, by both its ends, to the saw table at a suitable distance.

The workpiece is fed into the cut while being supported along its length by the waste acting as a guide. This method can be used as an alternative to the fence technique. It does provide a more easily guided base from which to work. The key for both lies in the accurate cutting of the first piece. Like the previous example many repeat cuts can be made at any required width.

A further development upon the same theme is to use single-point cutting, this time for the curved work. Once more the workpiece should be cut to the desired arc first. Set up the single-point support as you would for straight ripping. Feed the work into the cut just after contact has been made with the support.

The trailing edge will be cocked out to one side and is brought round as the cut proceeds. Again this is a great and easy way to produce lots of repeat curved work. In addition to one-way curves the single-point support technique has an advantage over all the others in that it can produce sequential curves in opposing directions. The cutting procedure is similar to all others; constant contact must be maintained with the crown of the single-point support as the cut proceeds. The trailing edge will be swung from side to side to accommodate the changing curve direction.

The combination of an offcut from a curved component and a single-point support can be usefully employed. Try this technique if consistent wider component work is needed. In the illustration on page 84 the waste is fixed back onto the workpiece. A special single-point support is made to 'shoot' over the workpiece to make contact with the waste that has become the pattern. The distance from the cutting edge to the pattern can be adjusted by altering the single-point crown position. Remember that like all other single-point cutting, the support should be available just before the cut commences. The workpiece is fed into the saw cut with the single-point crown on the leading edge. The trailing edge needs to follow round as the cut proceeds.

Many repeat components can be made using this technique, once the waste piece has been established as the pattern. It can be fitted to any number of stock boards at equal distances to produce the component over and over again, or can be used for one-offs. The single-point support

*Fig 112 Straight ripping using the single-point cutting technique.
Note the workpiece is just touching the rounded crown of the support
prior to the blade cutting.*

*Fig 113 Single-point straight ripping. Feed the workpiece through to produce
an equal cut, angling to one side or the other to compensate for blade 'lead'.*

Fig 114 With the wide support in place, the workpiece is held gently but firmly against it and is then fed into the saw cut, a useful technique for deep cutting.

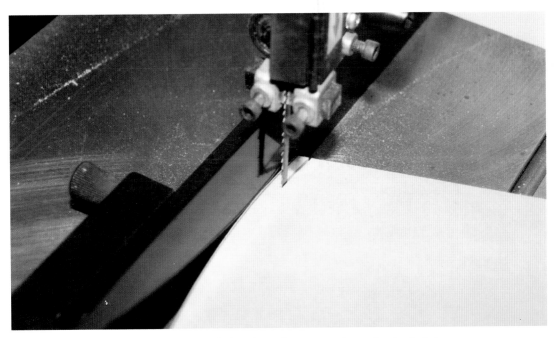

Fig 115 Using the fence, lead the workpiece into the saw cut just after its point of contact. The trailing end is cocked out to achieve this.

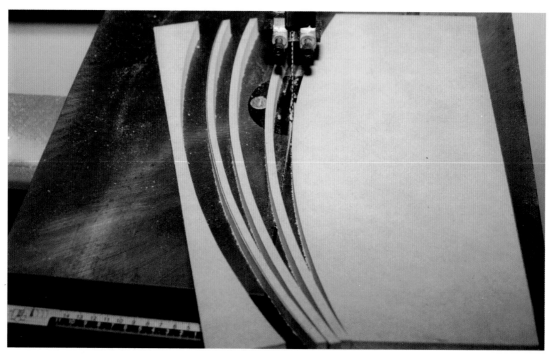

Fig 116 *Using the fence as a single-point can produce many equal pieces like this.*

Fig 117 *Run the workpiece against the curved fence made from the offcut and into the saw cut.*

Fig 118 With a single point, as the cut proceeds the trailing edge is brought round to follow the curve as the piece is fed through the saw.

Fig 119 Repeated curved rippings can be made using the single-point support technique.

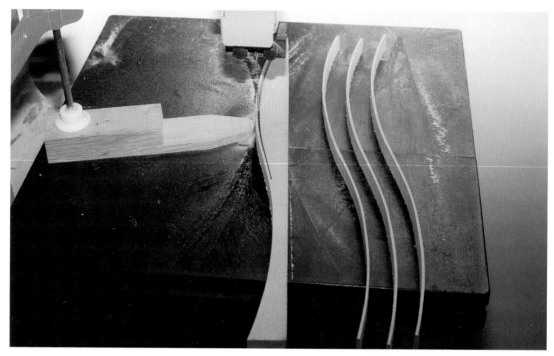

Fig 120 Sequential curved work can also be produced using the single-point method.

Fig 121 Use the offcut as a pattern from which the single-point support can work to produce consistent components.

Fig 122 In this case the single-point support overshoots the workpiece to rub upon and guide from the pattern fixed to it.

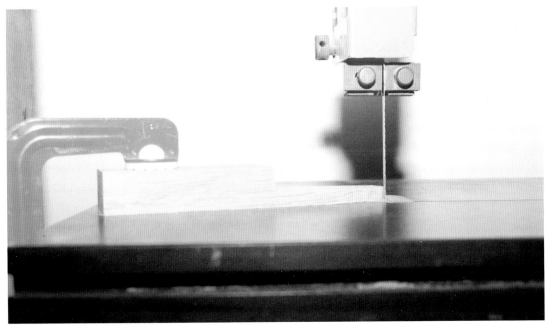

Fig 123 The overlapping single-point can be reversed for use in other applications.

Fig 124 With the single-point guide reversed you can revert to freehand cutting, in this case opposing curve work.

used in this exercise can be reversed to provide a point that produces rippings, etc., as described in the previous sections.

If faced with the likelihood of repeating irregular shapes, or working in a production-orientated environment another technique might help. It may well be worthwhile considering modifying your machine to enable it to use a 'guide pin' system. This technique is the next stage on from the single-point method described above and adopts the same work feed principles. Its advantage comes when related to the number of components required. If there are lots, then a pattern can be made from some hardened material – steel, say. These harder patterns should not lose too much of their integrity through prolonged use. For most general purpose workshops, unless the facility is already fitted, it is unlikely that the volume of work will justify this attachment.

CUTTING DISCS AND CONES

Most new machines come with the option of buying a disc-cutting attachment as part of the package. Although useful, they are not mandatory and I will be showing you how to make your own. First let's deal with the kit that might be supplied with the machine. Most will have some form of locking arrangement that fixes them to the bandsaw. Additionally they should be height-adjustable to allow for varying thicknesses of work and radius adjustable for the differing sizes of discs to be cut.

The best place in which to position the attachments point, around which the workpiece will be fed, is at right angles to the cutting edge of the blade. The radius can be measured for the desired circle from the blade edge to the point of the pin. Always allow a bit for cleaning up

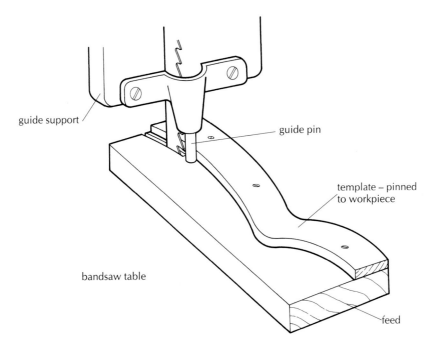

guide support

guide pin

template – pinned to workpiece

bandsaw table

feed

Fig 125 You may need to specially adapt your machine in some way to allow for the guide pin to be fitted for this type of work.

unless you are going to be satisfied with a sawn finish on the surface. Raise the pin clear of the workpiece, which you will have already marked with your circle and its centre. Feed the work into the saw free-hand, cutting to the outside of your line. At this point you should be able to drop the pointed pin into place in the centre of the disc. Some slight adjustment may be necessary in position and angle to do this, but practice will improve matters. Care should be taken to ensure that the pin is firmly in place, but not so tight that it is impossible to turn the workpiece around it. Now it is a simple process of feeding the work through the saw cutting action at a constant, comfortable pace.

Practice makes perfect, as they say. After a little while, once the first disc has been cut to your satisfaction, many more can be repeated without having to mark them out. If several are to be produced it is

helpful to cut them into rough squares first. Remember that the throat of your machine will not allow you to swing long lengths around the point while cutting.

Making your own disc-cutting device is fun, and can be quite easy. First, fit a strip of wood into the mitre gauge slot on your saw table. It should be a snug but not tight fit. Do not let the thickness of this strip protrude above the saw table surface. If it does, it will allow the board you will fit to it to rock, and that is not ideal. Taking any old bit of ply or composite board, as long as it is flat, fit the strip to it. This effectively becomes a false bed onto which your work-piece will be located.

With the strip fixed in place on the underside of your false bed, slide it into the mitre gauge slot and through the saw cut. This will establish the outside edge of the cut from which you can measure the radius of your desired circle. At right

Fig 126 Typical circle and disc-cutting kit supplied with many small bandsaw machines.

Fig 127 The disc-cutting attachment in place. The radius of the circle is determined by the distance between the attachment's point and the cutting edge of the saw.

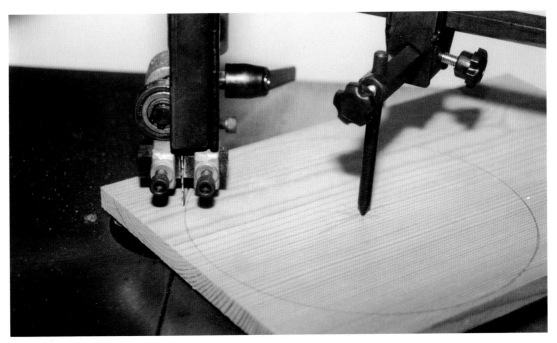

Fig 128 The workpiece is fed into the saw freehand until the cut is positioned just on the outer edge opposite the centre. Drop the attachments point into place and proceed to feed the workpiece into the cutting edge.

Fig 129 The finished disc cut just outside the pencil line to allow for cleaning up.

Fig 130 Any old bit of ply or composite board, providing it is flat, will do for the false bed. Fit the slat to it.

angles to the blade, mark a line down the centre of your false bed. This must be lined up with the cutting edge of the saw. Measuring along it, mark at the appropriate spot the required radius. With the false bed in place it is useful to fix a stop at the back side of it, against which it will come to rest with the centre line exactly opposite the saw cutting edge. Make sure the stop does not protrude above the false bed thickness. Having determined the radius you want and marked it on the centre line, pre-drill a small hole and knock a short nail or spike up through. This should be sharp and only needs to protrude about ⅛in (3mm) above the false bed surface.

Off the saw, locate your workpiece onto the pin. Swivelling it around will show you if it's big enough to cut the desired disc. Start the machine and mount the false table locating the strip into the mitre gauge slot. Feed the whole thing into the cutting edge until the bed comes up against the back stop. At this point the workpiece can be gently rotated. Continue the cutting action, turning the workpiece around the spike until the disc is cut right through.

If you are unfortunate enough not to have a mitre gauge slot in your saw table, then you will have to adapt this set up slightly. Use a false bed that overhangs the outer side of the saw table. A strip of wood is fitted to the bottom side to run along this extreme outer edge of the table. A little more care needs to be exercised when using this type of false bed. One hand will need to ensure that pressure is constantly applied to keep the strip up against the outer saw table edge. One good thing about it is that if you do let the false bed move a bit, it will only make the disc bigger, not smaller. If this should happen you can then run round it again to cut it to the correct size.

Using this type of home-made jig to cut conical-shaped pieces is a doddle, as it is of course with the proper attachments. Cut bowl blanks with a fair amount of waste removed before mounting on the lathe, or slope-sided plinths for mounting cups, etc. Decide upon the angle at which the sides of the discs will slope, and tilt the bandsaw table to suit. This may require a little thought and adjustment until the right pitch is found. Mount the centre of the blank on the sliding table spike. Remember that you will be viewing the larger diameter of the disc as you cut therefore aim to cut over-size rather than under in the first instance. Start the machine and feed the workpiece into the cutting edge as you would when cutting a straight-sided disc. When the centre point is reached, opposite the leading edge of the saw blade, start to swivel the blank around the

spike while holding the sliding table steady. You may find it easier to have a stop fixed to the saw table against which the sliding table is pushed to hold it firmly while cutting, as we did with the discs.

Continue to feed the workpiece right round at a pace at which the saw does not struggle, until the entry cut is met. Take the last bit of the cut steadily to ensure you have a smooth surface adjoining the entry and exit cuts. Turn the machine off before you attempt to lift out your handiwork. With luck and experience you will be able to produce disc blanks that require little further surface finishing.

I guess the key to mastering most of the skills in this chapter is confidence. With lots of this you will have a go at anything, but remember you can help yourself by ensuring you have the right blade and that it is sharp enough. In addition to this think out the way in which each job is going to be tackled and plan it through before you start.

Fig 131 Mark a centre line on the false bed at right angles to the blade. After determining the required radius, knock a sharp nail or spike up through onto which the workpiece will be located.

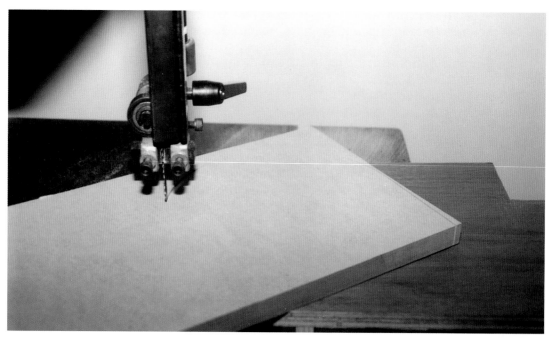

Fig 132 With the workpiece firmly fixed on the spike and in place, feed the false bed along the mitre gauge groove until it reaches the back stop, then start to rotate the component on the spike and on through the cutting action.

Fig 133 The completed disc is cut smoothly and efficiently even though the jig is home-made!

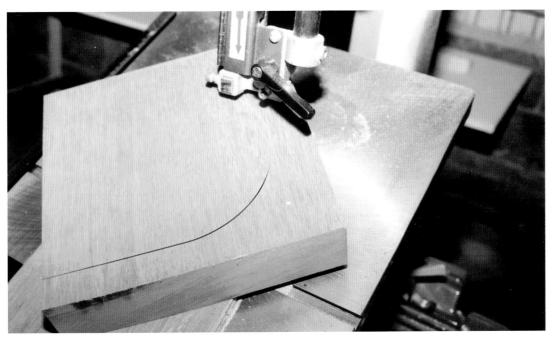

Fig 134 Cutting conical shapes. When the workpiece reaches the point in the middle, opposite the leading edge of the blade, start to rotate the blank gently on the spike.

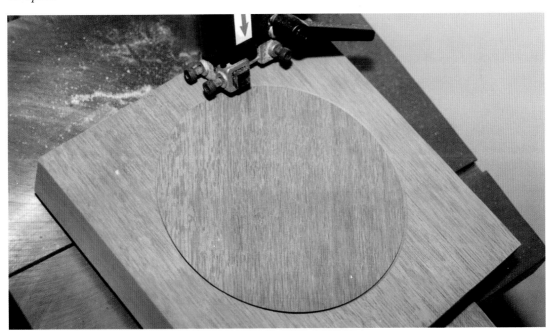

Fig 135 The cutting action continues right round until the entry point has been reached.

Fig 136 Turn the machine off before you start to disengage the bits and pieces. If all goes well you will end up with a perfect conical shape. (Try not to waste as much wood as I did in this example!)

CHAPTER six

USEFUL JIGS, CUTTING AIDS – AND SOME FUN

This chapter expands further upon the use of home-made jigs, cutting aids, more techniques and some novelty stuff. I personally believe that the small bandsaw is one of the most versatile machines available to the woodworker. Its functional use can be extended in lots of ways only restricted by the physical restrictions of depth of cut, throat width and blade type. The rest can be left entirely to the imagination and inventiveness of the operator.

JIGS AND AIDS

The home-made jig for discs that I described in the previous chapter can be further developed for use as a cross-cut and angle-cutting table. You will recall that the edge adjacent to the bandsaw blade was cut off parallel to it. A basic fence, made from a small batten, must be attached to the false table, against which the workpiece can rest during the cutting action. Simply fix this batten to the table with one central screw. You will need another screw positioned further back along the batten. This one will not be fixed until you have squared this fence from the leading edge. When this second screw has been driven home and the angle checked, work can commence. In this case the example shows some cross-cutting. A length stop has been fitted to the table; the stop has been chamfered back slightly on the edge adjacent to the fence. This allows the workpiece to fit snugly up against it every time. Waste and other debris will be unable to get between these two, and consequently altering the length slightly. A similar chamfer could be run along the front edge of the stop adjacent to the false table and also along the front of the fence if desired. Both will help avoid build up of debris, which could alter measurements. Common sense indicates that it is a good idea to clear any loose sawdust away on a regular basis.

This same jig can be converted into a sliding mitre table. Simply release the retaining screw and position the fence with a mitre square from the front edge. Refix the second screw and by cutting a bit of waste material, check that the angle is correct. To establish how accurate your mitre angle is, try the falling piece against the waste wood and use a square. It may be that some slight adjustment is necessary before the real work commences. You can ensure the fence returns to the correct position for each angle requirement. Mark in pencil along it on the false table and write the angle at the end of the line. If all things are equal, and you do not have a blade that 'wanders', you should be able to reuse this home-made sliding table over and over again.

For a lot of jig work you will need a table fence from which to work. One machine I have has the fittings, but for some reason I have never had the fence. Up until now I have always made my own fence, being too much of 'Scrooge' to go and buy one! If you need to make one, it is very simple. Take a bit of waste plywood or other composite material. It will need to be long

Fig 137 *Sliding table and fence assembly set up for repeat cross-cutting. The length stop is held in place with a G-cramp. Obviously this type of set up is not really suitable for long or very heavy workpieces.*

Fig 138 *Check that the mitre angles are correct by cutting a piece of waste. Make sure the waste has parallel sides and is of similar size to your workpiece.*

Fig 139 The easiest way to check if the mitre angle cut is at right angles is to invert the falling piece and check with a try square.

Fig 140 To square the table fence drive one screw home and set off a try square. Before final fixing try a bit of waste to make sure all cuts as it should.

enough and wide enough to provide support to the pieces you will fix to it. Use the bandsaw to shape it, then fix along the long side a piece of planed hardwood – sawn would be too rough for the workpieces to run along it. Glue and screw this piece in place, then fix on the bracket that is fitted below the ply at right angles to attach the fence to the saw table. Drive home a central screw first and square off the front edge of the saw table. Always run a test piece past the saw at this stage, to check the cutting action.

Finally fix the bracket in place with a second screw driven in from the top and a third right up through from the bottom. This last one should go through the corner into both bits of hardwood. To use the fence simply lock in place using a G-cramp or similar. As time goes on this fence will no doubt wear and need replacing. Using hardwood as the work surface should prolong its active life.

Some small bandsaws may not have a tilting table facility. This can be a bit of a pain if you wish to cut a lot of angles along the length of a workpiece. Maybe it is also rather a fiddly operation to keep resetting the angle of the saw table for repeat work. In these instances you may wish to make a sliding jig. A simple angled jig can be made from bits of waste ply, etc. A flat piece is used as the base onto which is fixed another piece at a predetermined angle. You will need to decide what that angle is going to be, and make a piece to fill in between the plywood. The example shown is fairly narrow. For dovetailing drawer sides, etc., a wider one would be more appropriate. When the jig has been made there are two modes of operation. If repeat past-the-saw cutting is required, the jig itself can be trimmed by passing through and cutting to width. With this done a width stop is fitted into place against which the workpiece runs, and cutting can commence.

If a wider jig has been made for cutting dovetails, use the table fence to adjust the position of saw cut, coupled with a stop behind the saw blade to regulate the depth. Clamp the jig in place while in use to avoid any slight movement that might alter the angles being cut.

A regular use for the small bandsaw is cutting tapers on legs. The jigs described here can be used just as well on a circular saw bench if you have one. The basic most simple way to approach this is by using an odd piece of waste as the former for the taper. First, mark the required slope of taper on one of the workpieces. Take a piece of waste wood or composite board, say, for argument's sake, 4inch (100mm) wide. Fix the table fence at a slightly lesser distance than the width of this piece. Run it through to make the sides parallel. Place the workpiece exactly on top of the jig blank with the taper overhanging the edge, and draw around it.

Remove the fence or move away to one side and then cut out the notched piece from the jig. Next reset the fence with the jig in place and the cutting edge just free from its side. This will allow a small amount of wood to be left on the workpiece, to plane off any saw cut marks afterwards.

Drop the workpiece into the pre-cut notch of the jig. Start the saw and move the whole thing, keeping it tight to the fence, into the cutting edge. Lead in gently and smoothly as the blade starts to cut. This will result in a much tidier entry point, and help with the cleaning up later. Continue to feed the workpiece through the cutting action until the job is complete.

If you are cutting a second taper, say to the inside of a leg, simply repeat the process by turning the workpiece over onto the next appropriate side.

The jig described here is the most basic and simple one for cutting tapers. You may decide that a more sophisticated and multi-adjustable version is more appropriate to

Fig 141 This simple fence assembly is easy to use, positioned and held in place with a G-cramp.

Fig 142 A jig used to produce repeated angle cuts along the length.

Fig 143 *The workpiece runs along the width stop that is fixed to the jig and is passed through the saw.*

Fig 144 *To make tapered cuts, first mark the workpiece with the required slope to be cut.*

Fig 145 With the table fence removed, carefully cut out the notch marked on the jig.

Fig 146 This example shows the tapered cut in progress. Feed the workpiece gently in at the point of entry to produce a smooth surface that will be easier to clean up later.

Fig 147 *Here you can see the tapered cut completed.*

your workshop. That being the case, make up one of your own. Even an adjustable jig will not take long to make. It has the advantage of being sufficiently adjustable to cope with most of the tapers needed in the workshop.

The simple taper jig forms the basic idea for a wedge-cutter. Take a piece of waste and run it to width with parallel sides. Mark in one end the size of wedge required and cut out the notch. The length of wedge will be determined by the specific job requirement – and it is a good idea to cut your blanks to the correct length right from the start. With the notched jig in place and the fence set, start up placing a blank into the notch. Pass through the machine to cut your wedge. Turn the blank over and pass through again repeating this until your fingers are getting too close to the blade, or you have cut enough wedges.

TENONS AND DOWELS

The small bandsaw's versatility comes into its own for some of the simplest of jobs. Tenoning is one of them, using standard attachments. I find it best to cut the shoulder of the tenons on a cross-cut first. There is no reason why this cannot be done on the bandsaw if you wish. Set the table fence so that the cut is on the outer side of the wide tenon face first. Use a length stop fixed to the table. This will ensure you do not mark the finished component by cutting too far.

Cut the two sides off the tenon by simply turning the workpiece over after the first cut. You will need to check the tenon for fit in your mortice now, before any others are cut. It is best to start too thick and thin them down if necessary. If you have a number of tenons to produce, cut all these wider faces first before re-setting the fence

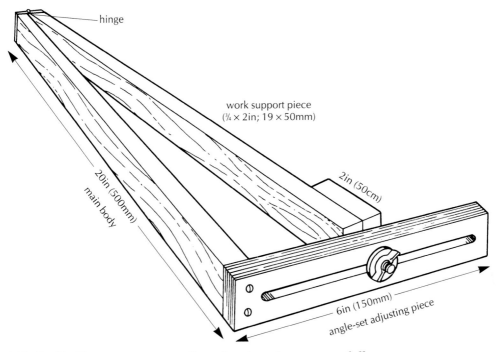

Fig 148 In this diagram you can easily see how to make your own fully adjustable taper jig.

Fig 149 To cut wedges, simply feed the blanks into the notch and through the saw. Turn the blank over after each cut – and keep your fingers out of the way!

Fig 150 With the fence set at the appropriate width of cut, use a length stop to ensure you do not cut back into the final component.

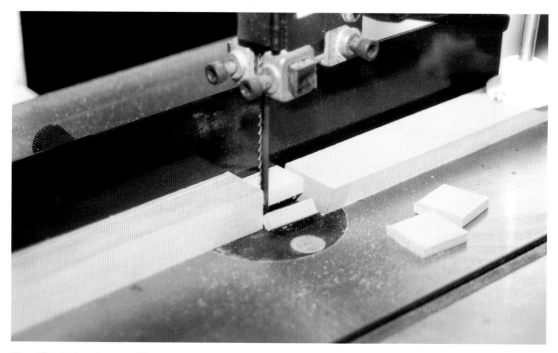

Fig 151 Trim the top off the tenon after altering the fence to suit. Note that the length stop is still in place.

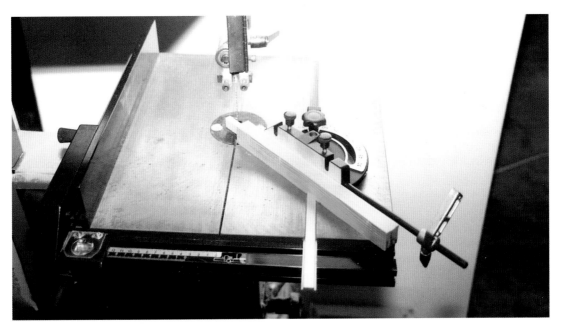

Fig 152 *To mitre tenons to fit into a corner post or leg, use the table fence and a mitre gauge. For consistency, use a length stop.*

Fig 153 *Making round tenons. The workpiece slides into the carriage along the groove and is easily controllable as it enters the cutting edge.*

to cut the tops and bottoms off. Leave the length stop in its original place.

If the waste to come off the tenon is not consistently of the same amount, for instance off each side, or off the top and bottom, you will need to set the fence three or four times to accommodate this. It may be that your tenons have to fit into rebates, or are going to be offset. If this is the case, always cut in sequence, all one side first, then all another, followed by the tops and bottoms, trying for fit as you go along.

If you are going to haunch the tenons, another couple of cuts and depth stop adjustments will be necessary. Mitre cuts on tenons that fit into a corner mortice joint can be cut with the sliding mitre gauge attachment. Simply set it up at 45 degrees and pass through the saw cut. Use a length stop for consistency. Failing that, set the table fence at the appropriate distance from the blade and push the component up to this before starting the cutting action.

On occasions you may find a need to handle lengths of round dowels or wooden rods. This may be simple cutting work, or perhaps reducing the overall diameter of the piece. It is always a good idea to hold round work firmly to avoid it spinning while being cut. If working along the length of a workpiece then make a carriage for it to rest in. In the illustration the workpiece rests in the 'V' and will be easy to control as it is pushed into the cutting edge. The carriage has been made from a piece of waste that has had a 45 degree groove cut into it on a circular saw bench. If you are unable to, or do not have, a circular saw that has the ability to tilt the fence or the arbour, you are not stuck. Make one up on the bandsaw by simply cutting two individual pieces and gluing them together.

When creating a round tenon to fit into a socket, the workpiece will need to be pushed into the cutting edge many times. As the cut proceeds, the waste will then be cut away. Use a depth stop fixed to the saw table, to determine how deep the tenon will be. Set the table fence at an appropriate distance from the blade to ensure that the size of the tenon is correct, and allow for a test run in case it is too small or large. If the first occurs you will need to cut the end off and start again, or in the second case just reduce the overall size by adjusting the table fence and carriage.

When the bulk of the waste has been removed by repeated cutting it is possible to finish off the job by rotating the dowel in the carriage along the length of the tenon. This will ensure that the overall finish on the reduced section has a smoother surface, with no high spots or ridges.

With all round work, some form of jig or carriage is useful to stop the workpiece moving during the cutting action. If perhaps you are cutting logs or odd-shaped pieces it is advisable to plane a flat surface to run on the saw table on one side before you start. By doing this you will avoid the possibility of the workpiece turning and distorting the blade during the cut. If this were to happen it would lead to undue stresses being applied, and possible breakages.

This same carriage can be used for diagonal cuts across the corners of a square. It will provide the necessary support to the workpiece to enable it to be held firmly during the cutting action. Feed the carriage into the saw cutting edge and beyond by about 1in (25mm) and then cramp it to the table. The workpiece can then be slid carefully up it and through the cut.

I turn a lot of home-made dowels for the furniture I make. Usually the materials used will match the timber from which the main piece is constructed and are therefore not readily available off the shelf. One problem with these dowels is that they do not have the small grooves found in the sides of commercially available dowels to release glue under pressure as they are driven in. To put your own small grooves in a dowel. Using a piece of waste, simply drill a vertical hole in it into which the dowel fits snugly. Set the table fence to produce a cut that runs into the middle of the hole. Drop the dowel into the jig and proceed to cut through until a groove is made in it.

One small groove is usually more than sufficient to release the pressure and allow the excess glue to escape. Longer lengths than those illustrated can be cut by lifting clear the guides, but beware of your fingers! Dowels also need cutting to length sometimes. The easiest way to do this is with the table fence and a mitre gauge. This may not be the most suitable of ways to cut short lengths, and you will find it easier to use the grooving jig instead. Set the fence at the required length and simply push the dowel into the hole and cut it off. You will need to withdraw the jig each time and push out the finished dowel. If this is too much trouble, there is an even simpler way. This uses a rebate cut into the bottom of a piece of waste. Rip the waste to width first, which probably determines the length of dowel. Cut a rebate for the dowel to fit snugly into and proceed to cut each one off. The advantage of this method is that each dowel blank can be pushed through the saw cut and left on the other side.

These are just a few jigs and cutting aids to get you started, I am sure the imaginative small bandsaw user will be able to multiply, expand and improve upon these in many ways and forms.

Fig 154 In this view the reduction has been completed; note the depth stop fitted to the saw table.

Fig 155 This is the finished job, showing the round tenon; it has been rotated in the carriage to remove any ridges.

Fig 156 Using the same carriage to cut squares across the diagonal.

Fig 157 With the dowel in place and the fence set, simply feed the jig into the saw cut until a slight groove has been cut into it.

Fig 158 An easy and quick way to cut short lengths of dowel is with a rebated piece of waste. The cut pieces are pushed out on the far side of the saw blade each time.

INTERNAL CUTS

On occasions it is necessary to make cuts internally. The only apparent way of achieving this is to break the blade and thread it through the workpiece, before re-joining the blade and commencing the cut. Afterwards the blade would need to be broken again and the work removed. This is what happens in some instances in the metal-cutting industry using special blades and butt jointers on the bandsaws. We discussed this briefly in Chapter 3. By capitalizing upon wood's elastic properties however, we can cheat a little.

An obvious internal cut is required when cutting blank letters from the alphabet up to make names, etc. Care needs to be taken when drawing the letters out to ensure they are in proportion. If you are likely to be doing a lot of this work, it is probably worthwhile investing in a set of patterns or make your own up. Once the letter has been outlined on the blank, you will need to determine the width of blade required to cut the smallest radius.

Study the letter and determine which will be the best and least obvious approach route for the blade to follow. When this has been decided make the initial cut into the letter and start cutting around the internal outline.

When you have finished cutting all the waste from the middle, switch off the machine and manoeuvre the blank back through the entry cut. At this stage you could remove some more of the waste from the outer profile but do not cut too much away. Now is the time to cheat! If your entry cut was straight and tidy and you did not try to cut your way back out, the two adjacent faces should fit back together nearly perfectly. Get some glue down into the joint and cramp it up.

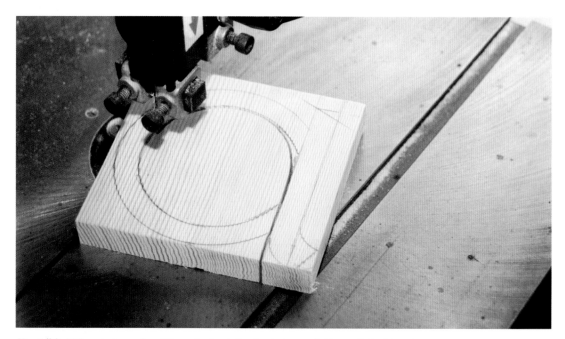

Fig 159 When internal cutting, look at the project carefully and decide upon the best and least noticeable entry cut; the blade should be of a width to suit the sharpest curve.

You will see now the reason for leaving some of the outer waste in place – it helps to cramp up what would normally be a difficult shape. When the glue has set, remove the cramp. Cut the rest of the outer profile and fill any small gaps with an appropriate wood filler. The final job can be sanded and cleaned up to produce what looks like a one-piece letter.

You will not be able to cut out middle waste like this every time. When you can try to remember not to design the width of your letters or profiles with sides that are too thick. The thinner they are, the more flexible the wood becomes.

HAVING SOME FUN!

Many years ago, as a young apprentice, I remember visiting a woodworking machinery exhibition in London. It was one of those organized trips from the local technical college. While we were there I was fascinated by the displays on small bandsaws. I cannot recall if they were praising the machine or the blades, but the operators dazzled us with their expertise. There was one demonstration that has always stuck with me. The operator took a block of softwood and drew around some templates onto it. With a very narrow blade he then proceeded to cut round the markings on three faces. All the cuts were quite well interlinked. Therefore not many bits of waste fell away during the process.

The culmination of this activity was a gentle tap on the saw table, removal of the waste, and from the midst of the block there appeared a model of a bird! We were all stunned of course – how could such a thing happen? Over the years I have tried at various times to replicate that performance. I have had some success, but not to the same degree that the expert had all those years ago. However, I thought it would be fun to produce a couple of examples for this book to help tone up your cutting skills. Perhaps they will whet your appetite to go on and 'carve' from wood using your own small bandsaw!

The principle is fairly simple: you work in three dimensions on a block of wood. For each of the dimensional views you have a template around which you draw the profile onto the block. You then cut round each profile in turn and, with luck, a finished or semi-finished model should appear. Some thought needs to be given to the sequence of cuts, to ensure you do not chop parts of the main model away as you go along. You also need some basic drawing skills to produce the templates, and a lot of imagination. The easiest way to explain is to show how it is done.

Starting with a simple swan: first, we need to prepare the profiles (scaled drawings are shown but do try and make some for yourself). To do this you will need to imagine what a swan would look like in full frontal profile. Some artistic licence is allowed – do not become bogged down in too much detail. The whole thing needs to be in proportion. In this case I decided to work with a block of cedar that measured 3¼in (80mm) wide, 4in (100mm) high and 6½in (160mm) long. Draw a side view in proportion, taking the previous template as a guide to where things such as head and wing height should come. Because it is fairly simple in this instance, we will be working with only two templates. The final cuts are made freehand and therefore will not need the top or plan view. When you are happy with your templates draw round them onto the block of wood ready for cutting.

Fit your bandsaw with a sharp, small or medium blade. In this case I used a ¼in (6mm) width blade. The first cuts are made with the block inverted. Standing 6in (150mm) in height, the cut will be made in line with the grain. Cut round the profile carefully and retain the waste.

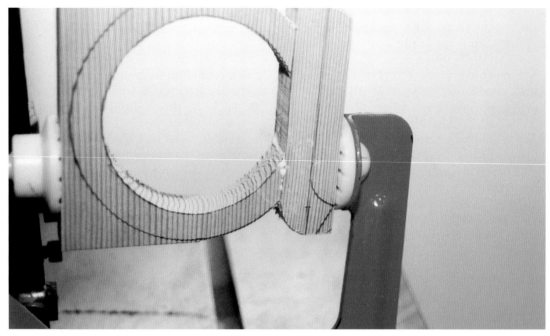

Fig 160 Cut out the internal profile and some of the outer profile. Work glue into the joint, cramp up and leave to dry. Note the usefulness of the remaining outer waste to aid cramping.

Fig 161 The final letter has been cleaned up, with little sign of the entry cut into the internal cavity.

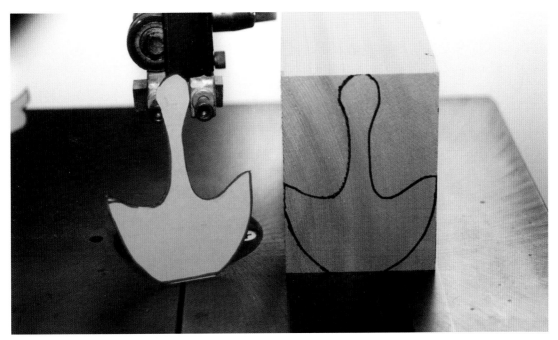

Fig 162 Mark the first profile on the end grain of the model block. It is a bit like the ugly duckling – things get better as you go along!.

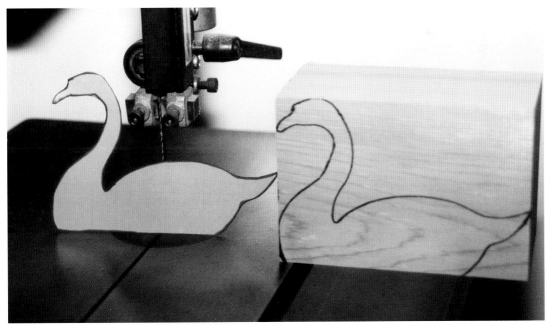

Fig 163 The second profile is marked onto the side of the block.

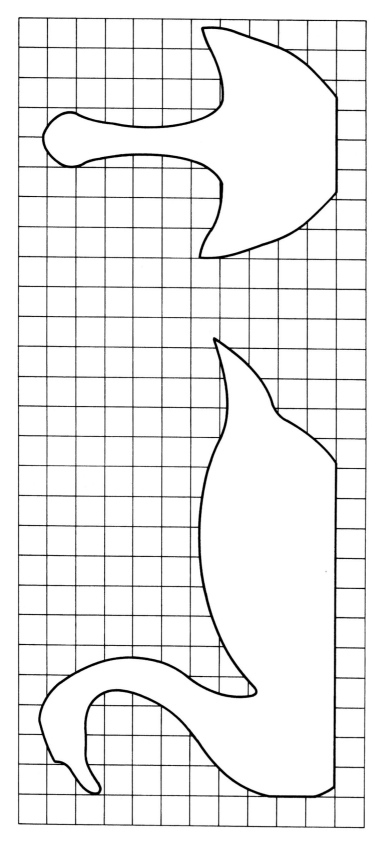

Fig 164 Template for the swan. Each square represents 1cm.

Fig 165 The first cuts are along the length of the grain of the block. The block stands 6½in (160mm) high like this. The blade must be of a suitable width and be sharp.

Try to exit from the cuts in as few places as possible, producing only a small number of waste pieces. When this is done you will find it necessary to stick back on the waste piece using some masking tape. Draw round the side profile again where the lines are missing.

Start the next stage by cutting away waste on the side that will not allow the block to fall to pieces before you have finished. Having done this, make a relief cut down into the corner at the base of the neck, then proceed to cut away the rest of the waste.

Clear away all the bits of waste and tape. At this point it does not look much like a swan – more like an ugly duckling! This is where you can start to put the 'art' into artisan. Take the model and cut the two outer profiles freehand, by eye. Think about the width of the beak at one end, the middle body and a pointed tail at the other, and cut away.

When the final outer profiles have been cut, the whole thing takes its final shape and looks good. If you wish to round off some of the corners, do so at this point with the appropriate carving chisels.

Just to prove that this was not a one-off bit of luck we will have a go at an elephant now. This block is cedar once more and measures 3½in (90mm) wide, 4in (100mm) high and 6in (150mm) long. The first cuts are made along the grain with the block inverted again.

With the first cuts made, stick the whole thing back together with masking tape. Draw round the template, marking over the missing bits. The same process is followed for the final series of cuts. Some of the waste will be getting too small to include at this point. For these final cuts the block needs to stand firmly on the saw table. This may be quite difficult at this stage, so take care.

When all the waste and tape has been removed your elephant will appear – or

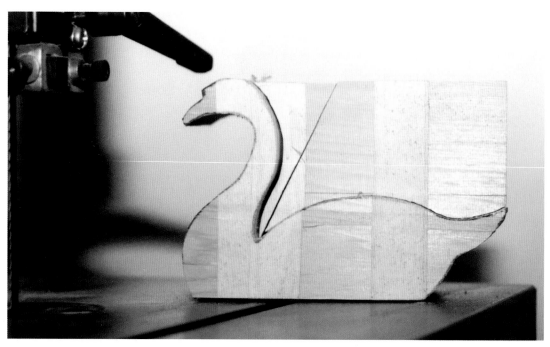

Fig 166 A relief cut has been made into the sharp corner prior to cutting away the last of the waste.

Fig 167 The swan after the first two-dimensional cuts, still looks pretty ugly!

Fig 168 Using your eye, and cutting freehand, cut away the two side profiles.

*Fig 169 The swan emerges from the waste and does not look too bad. Round off
some of the edges by hand now if you wish to do so.*

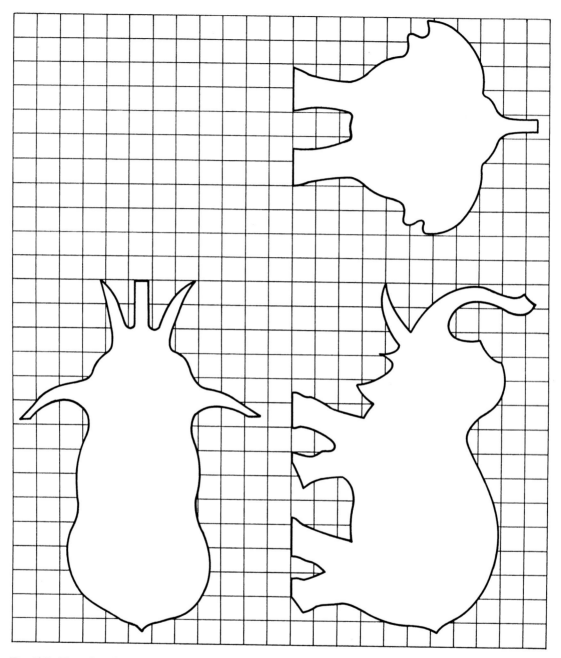

Fig 170 Template for the elephant. Each square represents 1cm.

will it? Well, I got a surprise – mine had eight legs, four tusks and a rather large mouth. I suppose it had to really, when you think about how it was cut. These 'extra'

bits need to be cut away by hand and with care, making sure you take off the right legs, leaving those that are still attached in order. Also take off the two top tusks and

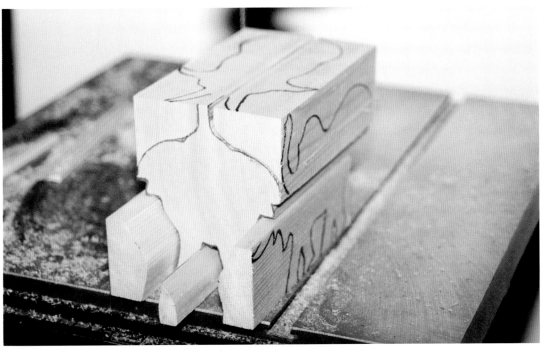

Fig 171 Like the other model, the first cut is with the block inverted and along the length of the grain.

Fig 172 The final series of cuts on the third dimension, from the top view, having again stuck the biggest bits of waste back on.

Fig 173 An elephant appears from the block; admittedly it has eight legs, four tusks and a large mouth!

Fig 174 Cut away the extra bits with care; make sure you get the right ones. Now it looks more like it should.

Fig 175 Front view of the finished elephant alongside the original template.

reduce the mouth. The final model looks pretty good to me, but I am sure with practice I could get even better at it.

The series of photographs show how close the actual profile achieved was to the original templates. A whole range of creatures could be carved with a small bandsaw if one put one's mind to it. The main requirements are an ability to think in three dimensions, ensuring nothing critical is cut off during the process, and making allowances for taking off some of the extra bits.

Apart from having the fun of making these models, there are some useful practical benefits to be gained by cutting in this way. Two-dimensional cutting can be used to produce table legs in a variety of forms. The only restriction upon design is your imagination. Cutting the models will also give useful practice when care and accuracy are required in the finished component.

Fig 176 A side view and template.

121

Fig 177 *The plan view of the elephant with the appropriate template.*

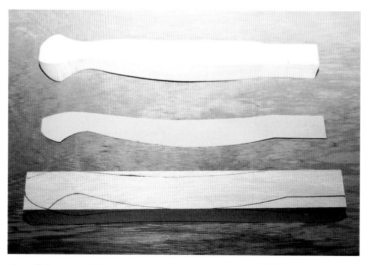

Fig 178 *In addition to having fun making models, the experience has practical uses when making and designing components such as this cabriole leg.*

Fig 179 *Template for a table leg. Each square represents 1cm.*

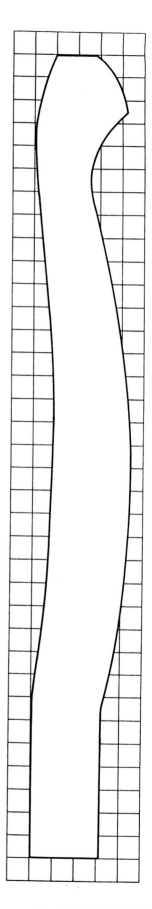

seven

HEALTH AND SAFETY

Maybe this chapter should have been at the beginning of the book, rather than nearer to the end, or possibly even at the beginning of each of the other chapters. I guess if we did that, however, you probably would not read the rest of it! Please remember that this subject has not been relegated to the end through lack of importance, I would like you to read it. If only one point sticks and makes you think now or in the future, it will have been worth it.

In Chapter 2 I started out by listing a few of the main points concerning safety while using a small bandsaw, most will be repeated again in this chapter. Common sense, I hear some say. Yes, that may be the case, but the problem we all have is that when using power tools we tend to get too familiar and careless, and that is when the trouble starts.

At the end of the chapter we have reproduced, with the kind permission of Her Majesty's Stationery Office, the full text and associated illustrations relating to the HSE leaflet: Safety in the use of narrow band sawing machines. Some of the information in this leaflet duplicates text elsewhere in the book, but I feel it does no harm to repeat it. For those who may have employees or others using their bandsaws it would be sensible to acquire the relevant leaflet and any other suitable material. You should make every operator read and understand it and then place it somewhere handy by the machine for future reference.

The following safety pointers are put together under some very broad headings

in no particular order and – yes – most of them are common sense really.

CLOTHING

- You should try to wear fairly tight or close-fitting clothes when using any machinery. Roll your sleeves up or button them up to avoid any trailing ends that might be caught in moving parts.
- If you have really long hair, tie it back out of the way. I can think of nothing worse than having your hair pulled into a machine.
- Remove any loose rings, bracelets or watch straps.
- Wear safety goggles or glasses and always keep them clean.
- Do not wear gloves – they may be caught in the blade and pull your hand towards it. In addition to this you will not be able to 'feel' how the machine is working.

WASTE

- Do not allow odd bits of waste to collect on or around the machine. It is good practice to clean up after every sawing job.
- Check inside the saw blade covers for any build up of dust; if it gets too thick it will create lubrication problems. If you can afford it, hook the machine up to an extraction system; this will additionally help remove a fair amount of dust from the air.

YOUR MACHINE

- Before you start, make sure you are conversant with every aspect of your machine. Read the instruction manual; it is there for a purpose.
- When setting the machine up, make sure it is fitted securely to a bench or stand and that it is levelled correctly prior to use.
- If you are not a qualified electrician, always get one to wire your machine up. Fit it with suitable isolation boxes or plugs that can easily be removed from their sockets, do not have trailing cables or wires all over the floor.
- Do not leave the machine turned on or running while not in use – someone else may inadvertently get hurt. Always switch it of at the isolation box, or remove the mains plug at the socket.
- Make sure you have selected the correct running speed for the timber and blade type.
- Do not try to cut a piece of timber that is too large either for you or for the machine to handle. If the machine is capable get help to hold one end or side. Your assistant does not need to control the cut, you can do that. This will save blades, guards, guides and maybe your fingers.
- Always set your top guide, thrust-bearing and guard assembly as close as possible to the surface of the workpiece. If you have to expose an extreme length of blade, make sure there is something between you and it.
- Do not take or leave off any of the guards or doors while the machine is running.
- Do not become distracted when using the machine. It is not a good idea to lock yourself in the workshop while it is running in case something does happen. Work out some sort of system to let others know when not to disturb you.

- Always keep children well away from any sawing activity and machinery.
- Replace saw table throat fillers, guides and thrust-bearings before they become totally worn out. Check the thrust-bearings for movement, and lubricate regularly.
- If you have tilted the table to make a cut, ensure the workpiece is supported by the table fence or another guide on the lower side of the blade.
- After resetting the machine do not leave loose tools lying around where they may interfere with or be caught up in the cutting action.
- Never operate machinery when under the influence of alcohol or drugs. You may not feel anything at the time, but you sure as hell will do later!
- Do not run your machine outside in the open, unless it is dry. Dampness or water ingress may lead to electrical failure or worse.
- When you have finished for the day make sure the machine cannot be turned on accidentally by another party. Disconnect it and lock it away.

BLADES

- If you think there may be a problem with a blade, take it off the machine and check it over. If you find any distortion or any fatigue cracking, you should not use it again.
- Remember to use the right blade for the job. Lots of ripping work will allow you to use a wider blade. Curved work will require a narrower blade appropriate for the radius being cut. If in doubt about which blade to use, always consult your supplier. They should have far more experience than most of us on correct blade selection.
- Keep your blades clean and sharp, they will perform much better for you if you do.

Fig 180 Use the push block for short and thin work. Push the workpiece through until the blade makes contact with it.

Fig 181 The 'feather' board in action. Use it in conjunction with a push stick.

- Tension and track the blades with the machine disconnected. When this has been done you can start and then stop the machine to see how the blade is running, before switching it on to run continuously.
- Do not force the workpiece through the blade, take it slowly to allow the waste to be removed. If you have an ongoing problem, check your blade for sharpness and consult your supplier.
- When a sawing operation has finished, wait until the blade has stopped moving and isolate the machine before you touch anything.
- If you have a braking device on your machine to stop the wheels from rotating, use it. Never apply side pressure to the blade to slow the wheels down.
- If a workpiece has become stuck or it is impossible to continue cutting, switch the machine off and wait for the blade to become static, before removing.

SAFETY AIDS

There are a few safety devices that you should consider using when appropriate. Flesh tends to cut pretty easily when it comes into contact with a saw blade. The trusty old push-stick is probably the most common around. Consider making a whole series of these that are long and short, thick or thin, to accommodate all the differing jobs you will be doing. Drill a hole in each one and hang it near the machine, ready for use.

Another useful tool is a push block fitted with a handle. This type is particularly good for thin or short work. The workpiece can be pushed through the cutting edge until the blade comes into contact with the block. It is a lot better than cutting your fingers. If you do not have a knob, fit the block with a square of wood or even an old plane handle.

A 'feather' board can be useful when doing a lot of ripping work. It also avoids those inevitable splinters you get when holding a workpiece against the fence as it goes through. It should be set to make light contact with the workpiece just in front of the cutting edge of the blade. Always use a push-stick with the feather board.

I have heard some say that these feather boards act as an 'anti-kickback' device. I guess to the uninformed that might appear to be the case. Because the cutting action of a bandsaw is down onto the saw table, they do not actually do this. The action of the bandsaw is fairly safe, unlike a circular rip saw bench that aims to throw the workpiece back at you, given half the chance! Anti-kickback devices can be found on most larger circular saw rip benches and radial arm saws, where they are a most useful safety aid. You will find it difficult to remove your workpiece back towards you if the feather board is set up correctly, as the fingers naturally tend to dig in. To get it out, push it on through the cut or lift it out and back, after turning the machine off.

GENERAL

Working with wood while using machines creates a tremendous amount of dust, although this may not be immediately apparent. If you have a problem related to breathing or your lungs, it is well worth considering a full-face respirator. These will eliminate all but the finest dust and allow you to breathe more easily. In addition to any breathing disorders, please remember that some wood dust is carcinogenic. It is always good practice to wear some sort of face mask to filter out the worst. I wear one all the time and it never ceases to amaze me how much dust the mask collects. I only wish someone would come up with a way of stopping my glasses from misting up, though!

SAFETY IN THE USE OF NARROW BANDSAWING MACHINES

The following is reproduced from the Health and Safety Executive's Woodworking Sheet No 31. Crown copyright is reproduced with the permission of the Controller of Her Majesty's Stationery Office.

INTRODUCTION

This information sheet is one of a series produced by HSR's Woodworking National Interest Group. Its purpose is to give practical guidance on safe working practices when using narrow bandsaws (blades <50mm in width) for curved and irregular work, circular work, bevel, tenon and wedge cutting and without a fence.

Legal requirements covering the use of these machines are contained in the Woodworking Machines Regulations 1974, and the Provision and Use of Work Equipment Regulations 1992.

This guidance is issued by the Health and Safety Executive. Following the guidance is not compulsory and you are free to take other action. But if you do follow the guidance you will normally be doing enough to comply with the law and may refer to this guidance as illustrating good practice.

ACCIDENT HISTORY

In a study of 1,000 accidents at woodworking machines, 4 per cent occurred on narrow band sawing machines. Most resulted from contact with the moving blade while presenting material to the blade or removing it from the table. Accidents also occurred while setting, cleaning, adjusting and maintaining the machine while the blade was still in motion.

GUARDING

The pulleys and the blade, except the part which runs downwards between the top pulley and the machine table, should be enclosed by substantial guards.

An adjustable guard should be provided to cover that portion of the blade between the top pulley and the machine table. This guard should be attached to and moved with the top sawing blade guide. It should be capable of being easily adjusted to suit the height of the workpiece and firmly secured in position.

The part of the blade between the underside of the table and the lower guide should be guarded at all angles of table tilt.

MACHINE SETTING

For a narrow band-saw to cut accurately and efficiently the blade type and width should be suitable for the material being cut, the blade teeth sharp and properly set, the blade correctly tensioned and tracked and the maximum thickness of blade suitable for the pulley wheel diameter.

TENSIONING

A saw keeps its condition longer if the tension on the blade is relaxed after use, eg at the end of a working period. A notice should be placed on the machine to indicate this and to remind the next user to adjust the tension before starting the saw.

TRACKING

Tracking helps the blade run in the correct position on the band-saw pulleys. This is achieved by tilting the top pulley.

When tracking, the thrust wheels and guides should be clear of the blade to allow it to move freely. With the machine isolated, the top pulley should be rotated by hand and the pulley tilted until the blade runs in the correct position.

With the guides and thrust wheel correctly positioned and the guards in the close position, run the machine under power. If the blade does not run correctly when under power, the manual tracking should be repeated. After tracking, the tension of the blade should be rechecked.

SAW BLADES AND THRUST WHEELS

The saw blade guides, which can be fixed pads, pegs or rotating rollers, should support the blade behind the gullets. They should not grip the blade but should support it during cutting.

The thrust wheels give support to the blade when cutting. They should be positioned in line and just clear of the back of the blade when the blade is idling after being tensioned and tracked. Lack of clearance will cause grooving of the thrust wheels and lead to blade failure.

MACHINE OPERATION

The saw guides and attached adjustable guard should be adjusted as close to the workpiece as possible before machining and kept in place during machining.

POWER FEED

Use a demountable power feed wherever possible, eg when cutting with a fence. This will remove the need for close approach to the blade by the operator and increase the output of the machine. By maintaining a constant feed rate, the device helps to prolong the working periods between blade sharpening (*see* Fig a).

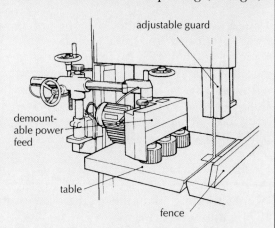

Fig a Narrow band saw with demountable power feed.

CUTTING WITH A FENCE

Always use a fence for straight cutting to prevent the workpiece rocking or sliding (*see* Fig b). For shallow work, use a low position fence to allow the blade guides and guard to be adjusted down to the workpiece and also to permit safe removal of material from the blade using a push stick.

When hand feeding against a fence use a wooden guide block to exert an even pressure on the workpiece. Use a push stick for feeding close to the blade (*see* Fig b).

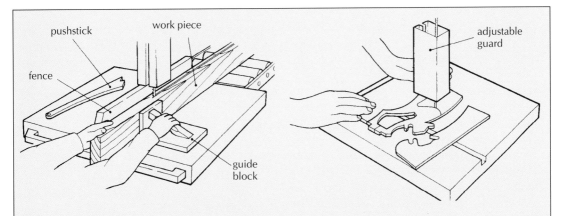

Fig b Straight cutting.

Fig d Freehand cutting.

CUTTING WITHOUT A FENCE

Where it is not practicable to use a fence, the workpiece should be led forward evenly (without exerting excess pressure) and held firmly on the table to ensure effective control during cutting. The hands should be kept in a safe position (*see* Fig c) by keeping them as far away from the blade as possible. When hands are unavoidably near to the blade they should be placed on either side of the blade, not in line with it (*see* Fig d).

CURVED OR IRREGULAR WORK

A variety of curved or irregular shapes can be produced with or without a template (*see* Fig d).

For repetitive work, a guide fixed in front of the blade used with a template improves safety as well as the speed of operation (*see* Fig e).

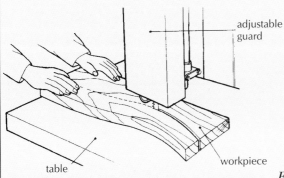

Fig c Handling shaped work on a narrow band saw.

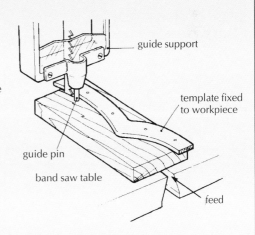

Fig e Cutting irregular shapes on a narrow band sawing machine using a template and guide.

BEVEL CUTTING

Bevel cutting is usually done by tilting the table, which means that additional workpiece support, such as a fence, is required to prevent the workpiece falling from the table. On machines with a fixed table or tiltable fence a jig is necessary to provide support for the workpiece. Push sticks should be used at the end of the cut (*see* Fig f).

Diagonal cuts on square stock can be achieved by feeding the workpiece through a trough-type of jig fixed to the the table (*see* Fig g).

CUTTING TENONS

Simple tenons can be cut (*see* Fig h). For complex tenons or repetitive work, jigs provide the safest system of work.

WEDGE CUTTING

Small wedges can be cut safely using the holder shown in Fig i.

CIRCULAR WORK

A jig for cutting circular discs is shown in Fig j.

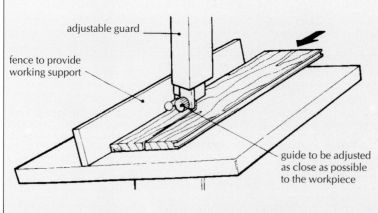

adjustable guard

fence to provide working support

guide to be adjusted as close as possible to the workpiece

Fig f Bevel cutting using a tilting table.

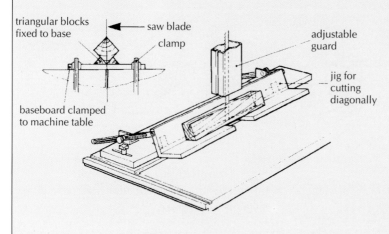

triangular blocks fixed to base

saw blade

clamp

baseboard clamped to machine table

adjustable guard

jig for cutting diagonally

Fig g Diagonal cutting.

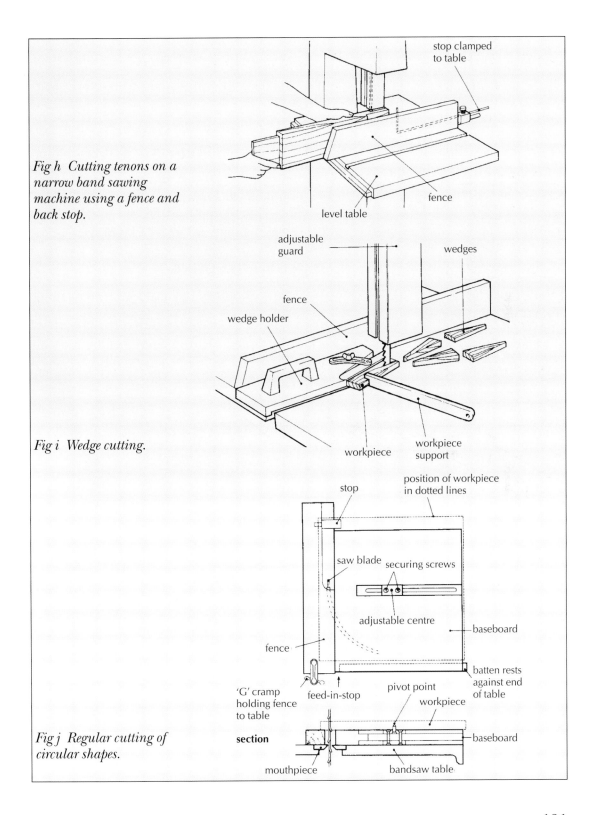

Fig h Cutting tenons on a narrow band sawing machine using a fence and back stop.

stop clamped to table

fence

level table

Fig i Wedge cutting.

adjustable guard

wedges

fence

wedge holder

workpiece

workpiece support

position of workpiece in dotted lines

stop

saw blade

securing screws

adjustable centre

baseboard

fence

batten rests against end of table

'G' cramp holding fence to table

feed-in-stop

pivot point

workpiece

Fig j Regular cutting of circular shapes.

section

baseboard

mouthpiece

bandsaw table

131

The workpiece is placed centrally on the pivot, with one edge touching the saw blade, and rotated to produce a circular disc. The cut should start on the end grain and the workpiece should be fed slowly with even pressure.

CROSS-CUTTING OR RIPPING ROUND STOCK

The workpiece will need to be secured to prevent rotation, caused by the cutting pressure. It should be held in a suitable jig or holder. The blade should be suitable for cross-cutting.

WORKPIECE SUPPORT

The table should support the whole workpiece. When a workpiece overhangs the table it should be supported using extension tables or roller trestles at both infeed and outfeed. Tipping of the workpiece is a common cause of accidents.

SAFETY DEVICES

Guide blocks should be used when hand feeding against a fence and push sticks used for feeding timber close to the blade and removing cut pieces from between the saw and fence.

CLEANING AND MAINTENANCE

Never clean the blade or pulley with a hand-held brush or scraper while the blade is in motion. Careful adjustment and regular maintenance of blade and pulley cleaning equipment will ensure resin residues will not build up.

A routine maintenance schedule should be drawn up to include for example blade condition, pulley bearing wear, pulley wear, correct operation of guides and thrust wheels, blade tensioning device, blade and pulley cleaning equipment, guards and safety devices.

TOOL SELECTION

The correct width of saw blade should be selected by measuring the smallest radius of any curve to be cut. Machinists should choose the widest blade which will cut this curve without bending. Excessive blade twisting may cause blade breakage.

TOOL HANDLING

Care shoud be taken to avoid damaging the saw blade. When not in use, narrow band-saw blades should be coiled into thirds and secured. Store blades in a safe dry place and before use check for damaged teeth and cracks. Transport blades in jigs.

TRAINING

Everyone who works at a woodworking machine must be familiar with the requirements of the Woodworking Machines Regulations and operators of band sawing machines should be trained in:

- principles of machine operation, correct use and adjustment of the tilting table, fence, jigs, holders and templates;

- selection of the correct blade for the operation, the set of the teeth, tensioning and tracking of the blade;

- safe handling of the workpiece when cutting and position of the hands relative to the blade;

- correct adjustment of the top guide and guard and blade guard below the table.

one

EXTRACTS FROM BSI 4411:1969 (1986)

The following extracts are reproduced by kind permission of BSI. Complete editions of the standard can be obtained by post from BSI Customer Service, 389 Chiswick High Road, London W4 4AL.

BS4411:1969 BRITISH STANDARD SPECIFICATION FOR WOODCUTTING BANDSAW BLADES

FOREWORD

This British Standard has been prepared under the authority of the Mechanical Engineering Industry Standards Committee, in an attempt to provide detailed information for both the users and the manufacturers of bandsaw blades.

The standard relates to both narrow and wide bandsaw blades, includes details of set, tooth shape, blade dimensions, blade material and running speeds; a fairly comprehensive list of terms have been defined, in order to provide a vocabulary common to the users and the manufacturers.

In the case of wide bandsaws, tooth shape has been related to the density of timber being cut, as this was felt to be the most general classification method available. In this connection it should be noted that this standard specifically excludes bandsaws suitable for cutting synthetic material. Teeth tipped with hard metals and double cutting bandsaw blades have also been excluded, as it was felt that they should not be considered as a standard item.

Attention is drawn to the fact that the cutting efficiency of band saw blades must depend to a large extent on the skill of the user in choosing the correct combination of tooth shape, blade width, thickness, pitch, machine wheel diameter, and speed, from those values shown in this standard. In case of doubt, the Forest Products Research Laboratory and/or manufacturers should be consulted.

It should be noted that only blades made to inch dimensions are available at present, but it is expected that their metric equivalents will gradually be phased-in. It is for this reason that inch units have been included in this standard, but only in an appendix in order that their use is not encouraged. The values quoted are compatible to achieve the same degree of accuracy, but are not exact mathematical equivalents.

SPECIFICATION

1. SCOPE

This British Standard relates to the terminology, manufacture, properties, dimensions and tolerances of both 'narrow' and 'wide' bandsaw blades; either supplied in coil, or cut to length and joined ready for use. The blades specified in this standard, which does not include blades tipped with hard metals, are suitable for cutting timber in its naturally occurring form, but not its manufactured derivatives (i.e. plywood, blockboard, or any synthetic material).

2. NOMENCLATURE AND DEFINITIONS

For the purpose of this British Standard the following definitions apply.

2.1 General

(1) *Narrow bandsaw blade.* A bandsaw blade which has a width not exceeding 65mm (2½in), and normally runs on a wheel covered by a tyre made of resilient material.

(2) *Wide bandsaw blade.* A bandsaw blade which has a width greater than, or equal to 80mm (3in), and normally runs direct on the metal base of the wheel, and is processed to ensure correct tracking of the band on the wheel.

(3) *Minimum cutting radius.* The radius of the arc of the smallest curvature that can be followed by a narrow bandsaw blade of given width.

2.2 Elements

To promote the fullest understanding of the various elements they are illustrated in Fig 182.

(1) *Body.* That part of the blade between the bottom of the gullet and the back edge.

(2) *Teeth.* The serrations formed along one longitudinal edge of the blade to provide the cutting edges.

(3) *Toothed edge.* The longitudinal edge along which the teeth have been formed.

(4) *Cutting edge.* The transverse edge formed by the intersection of the back and the face of the tooth.

(5) *Face.* That surface of the tooth adjacent to the cutting edge, on which the chip impinges as it is severed from the work.

(6) *Back.* That surface behind the cutting edge which extends to the root radius of the gullet.

(7) *Sharpness angle.* The angle between the face and the back of the tooth, at the tooth point.

(8) *Clearance angle.* The angle between the back of the tooth, at the tooth point, and the cutting path.

(9) *Gullet angle.* (for narrow blades only). That angle, in the gullet, between the

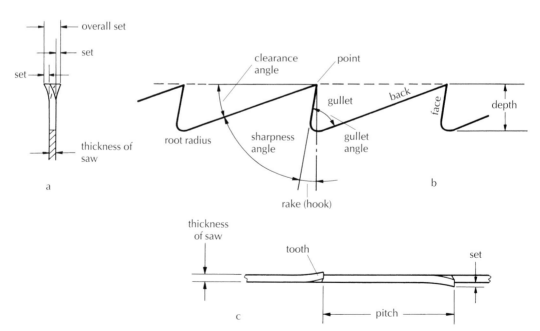

Fig 182 Narrow bandsaw tooth profile.

front and the back of the tooth.

(10) *Rake (Hook)*. The angle between the face of the tooth before setting, and a line from the tooth point at right angles to the cutting path.

(11) *Depth*. The distance from the point of the tooth to the deepest part of the gullet, in a direction at right angles to the cutting path.

(12) *Root radius*. The radius of the arc between the face and the back in the gullet.

(13) *Gullet*. The space bounded by the face, root radius and back of a tooth, to contain severed chips.

(14) *Set*. The projection of the teeth from each side of the blade to provide cutting clearance.

a. *Spring set*. The transversant setting of alternative teeth as shown in Figs 182a and b.

b. *Swage set*. The spreading of the metal at the point of the tooth (*see* Fig 182c).

(15) *Overall set*. The sum of the set on either side of the blade and the thickness of the blade itself.

2.3 Linear dimensions

(1) *Width*. The overall distance between the point of the tooth and the back edge.

(2) *Thickness*. The distance between the two sides of the body of the blade.

NOTE. Birmingham wire gauge is often used at present as a measure of thickness.

(3) *Pitch*. The distance between the points of two adjoining teeth, expressed as:

a. mm (or teeth per inch) for narrow blades

b. mm (or inches) for wide blades.

FAULT-FINDING CHART

The following chart is reproduced by kind permission of Slack Sellars & Co. Ltd.

PROBLEMS	CAUSES	SOLUTIONS
Premature wearing of teeth	1. Band speed too fast. 2. Teeth not cutting merely rubbing. 3. Tooth pitch too coarse. 4. Band and materials over-heating. 5. Band teeth running in wrong direction.	1. Reduce band speed. 2. Increase feed pressure. 3. Select finer pitch. 4. Apply a copious supply of coolant. 5. Replace band correctly.
Excessive band vibration whilst cutting	1. Unsuitable band speed. 2. Incorrect cutting pressure being used. 3. Band pitch too coarse. 4. Movement of material whilst being cut. 5. Insufficient band tension.	1. Increase or decrease according to section, size and type of material being cut. 2. Decrease or increase according to size being cut. 3. Select finer pitch. 4. Hold/clamp material firmly. 5. Adjust band tension.
Bandsaw teeth stripping	1. Tooth pitch too coarse for section being cut. 2. Excessive feed pressure. 3. Band teeth approaching sharp corner on the material being cut. 4. Material insecurely held. 5. Gullets choked with swarf.	1. Select finer pitch. 2. Reduce feed pressure. 3. If possible present a flat surface to the band when starting to cut. 4. Hold/clamp material firmly. 5. Apply suitable coolant.
Rough surface finish of section being cut	1. Tooth pitch too coarse. 2. Band speed too slow. 3. Feed rate too great.	1. Select finer pitch. 2. Increase band speed. 3. Decrease feeding rate.

PROBLEMS	CAUSES	SOLUTIONS
Bandsaw breakage	1. Band tension too great.	1. Decrease band tension. Ensure that band tension is released when not in use.
	2. Feed pressure too great.	2. Decrease feed pressure.
	3. Tooth pitch too coarse.	3. Select finer brand.
	4. Maladjusted guides.	4. Adjust correctly.
	5. Machine driving wheels at fault.	5. Periphery of wheels are free from defects.
	6. Band running too fast.	6. Decrease band speed.
Bandsaw making bow-shaped cut	1. Feed pressure too great.	1. Decrease band feed pressure.
	2. Insufficient guide support to band.	2. Adjust guides as close as possible to material being cut.
	3. Pitch too fine.	3. Select coarser tooth pitch.
	4. Insufficient band tension.	4. Increase band tension.
Gullets of bandsaw teeth choked with swarf	1. Tooth pitch too fine.	1. Select coarser pitch.
	2. Lack of coolant.	2. Apply liberal supply of suitable coolant.
	3. Band speed too fast.	3. Decrease band speed.
Bandsaw running out of square in cut	1. Maladjusted bandsaw guides.	1. Re-align bandsaw guides – if worn replace.
	2. Excessive feed pressure.	2. Reduce feed pressure.
	3. Uneveness in material being cut. Inclusions in material being cut.	3. Generally decrease cutting rate.

GLOSSARY

Annealing The process that restores the correct hardness and strength to the bandsaw blade by re-heating it and cooling it slowly.

Bandmills A combination of various types and sizes of bandsaw used in one location to convert logs into lumber.

Binding When a bandsaw blade is forced around a radius that is too tight for it to operate efficiently, the back edge of the blade will bind in the saw cut. Binding also refers to the instance when the saw cut is too narrow and the wood pinches on both sides of the blade. This is most likely to be caused by the timber having been dried incorrectly.

Blade A bandsaw blade is a continuous coil of steel with cutting edges on one or both sides.

Butt/resistance welding A mechanical method for jointing bandsaw blades. Mounted in a purpose-made machine the two ends of the blade are heated and moved together, forming the joint as they fuse.

Carriage Logs are mounted onto carriages when they are being converted in a bandmill. On some sort of track the log can be held firmly and safely in place and passes by the bandsaw during the cutting action.

Deeping Cutting timber along its length up on its edge through the widest dimension.

Feed speed The speed at which the workpiece is fed through the machine during the cutting action. How fast you go will be determined by the size of motor, speed of blade, type of blade and so on.

Flat wheels Found on most small bandsaws. These flat wheels will probably be fitted with a rubber tyre to protect them from the saw blade teeth. The blade is tracked to run correctly by adjusting the angle at which the top wheel runs.

Flexi-back A type of saw blade that has a softer steel blade back and hardened teeth. These blades cannot generally be rejointed after breakage.

Flexing The term used to describe unwanted movement between the top and bottom wheels. Too much flexing will fatigue blades, leading to breakage and will also not lend itself to continuity of cut.

Forms The shape of the saw tooth. Each is designed for optimum cutting under particular circumstances.

FpM Feet per minute is the speed at which the saw blade travels.

Frame The frame is the structure from which the bandsaw is built. It may be made up from a cast or from welded components. The strength and rigidity of the frame will help to determine the life of blades used. Too much flexing will lead to premature fatigue in the blades.

Green Very wet or fresh, recently cut wood from a tree trunk. Usually a lot easier to cut that dry wood. Bigger teeth can be employed on the blade, aiding waste removal and leading to faster feed speeds.

Gauge The thickness of the saw blade body.

Guide assembly Two sets of adjustable saw blade guides. One set is fixed below the table and the other above on a sliding post. Both sets combine two side support blocks with, generally, a thrust bearing at the rear.

Guide pin A pin fixed to the top sliding guide assembly post from which repeat patterns are cut.

Gullet Part of the saw tooth. This is the cavity into which the sawdust is deposited for removal from the cut.

Headrig In bandmills, conversion from log to lumber, the first cutting and largest bandsaw is generally called the headrig saw.

Hook Part of the saw tooth. The design of the tooth point angle in relationship to the rake and gullet angles.

Jigs Any useful cutting aid that allows the workpiece to be handled or cut more easily.

Kerf The width of cut made in the workpiece. This is determined by the amount of set the saw teeth have to each side, creating clearance for the saw body.

Mitre gauge A sliding gauge/fence assembly that usually fits into a groove in the saw table. Used for cutting a wide variety of angles across the grain of the workpiece.

Nibbling A technique used during cutting to create more side clearance in which an oversize blade can operate.

Pitch The number of teeth per inch on a saw blade.

Point The point or cutting edge of the saw blade, the leading edge. The sharpness of this will be determined by varying angles related to it and also the type of material being cut.

Push block A safety device that provides contact with the workpiece along an extended face.

Push stick Another common safety device that allows you to push through a workpiece using one narrow point of contact on it.

Rake The angle at which the face of the teeth are cut from the body of the blade. Normally this is at 90 degrees and is known as 'zero degree' rake. If it is increased to create a hook effect it is then called 'positive rake'.

Resaw A medium sized bandsaw normally with mechanized feed works. Used in many sawmills for conversion of timber into smaller sizes, hence the name resaw.

Ripping Cutting timber down the length of the grain through the thinner dimension, not up on its edge.

Set The amount each tooth on the saw blade is alternately 'set' to one side or the other. This creates the kerf, clearance, in which the blade body can operate freely.

Side clearance The amount of set to one side of the blade body. Together, both sides create the kerf.

Side support Part of the saw guide assembly, the two side blocks providing support to the sides of the blade.

Single point cutting A technique using a sawing aid/jig that provides a single point from which the workpiece finds support and guidance during the cutting action.

Skip tooth A specialist type of saw blade configuration; as the name suggests, every other tooth is missing. Especially useful when faster cutting can be achieved or with wet timbers and soft metals.

Sliver steel A type of steel used in the body of the saw blade that allows it to be jointed using simple brazing techniques.

Spring set Saw teeth that are alternately bent to each side to create individual side clearance, which combined becomes the kerf of the saw blade.

TPI Number of 'teeth per inch'.

Table The saw table. A level surface that can be set at various angles to the cutting blade and provides the necessary space and support for the workpiece.

Table fence An adjustable fence usually on a sliding bar or in a groove attached to the saw table to provide support to a workpiece during the cutting action.

Template Any reusable profile made from plywood, plastic, hardboard and so on. For jobs where it is likely the project will be repeated it is a good idea to make these and keep them for future use.

Tensioning Applies pressure to the bandsaw blade thereby placing it under tension. Sloppy, loose saws will not perform correctly, over-tensioning may damage the frame of the machine. When not in use tension should be released from the blade to avoid over-stressing it or the bandsaw frame.

Throat The width between the inner edge of the bandsaw frame on the one side and the edge of the blade nearest to it on the other. This measurement is sometimes used to describe the size of the machine. A three-wheeled bandsaw is likely to have a larger throat than a two-wheeled one, depending upon the size of the wheels.

Throat piece A removable section in the bandsaw table that aids blade removal. It is usually made of wood or plastic and therefore has another use in preventing the blade from touching the metal table.

Thrust-bearing Part of the guide assembly, the thrust-bearing is usually to be found giving support to the back of the blade. By turning, it helps to disperse any heat build-up; if it is seized up it must be replaced or damage to the blade will result.

Tilting table Most bandsaws have a table with this facility, the ability to tilt to allow various angles to be cut.

Tracking Combined with tensioning, the tracking of the blade is of paramount importance to its cutting performance. Usually the blade is set to the right track, the position in which it travels round the wheels, by canting the top wheel forwards or backwards.

Turning holes A technique used with small blades to turn in the workpiece without exiting from it. Useful when cutting up to a point within an intricate design.

Wheels The two or three wheels on the bandsaw that the blade runs around. Generally speaking the two-wheeled machines are more robust but the three-wheeled machines usually have a greater throat capacity.

Width of cut This refers to the widest possible cutting point between the frame of the bandsaw and the nearside of the blade, normally described as the throat width.

Yield The amount of 'good stuff' produced during any cutting operation. Usually used as a phrase to describe how much useful material has been cut from the whole of a log.

FURTHER READING

British Standards Institution *Safeguarding Woodworking Machines* BS 6854 Part 5:1989 *Narrow band sawing machines.*

Specification for Woodcutting Bandsaw Blades BS 4411:1969.

Training Woodworking Machinists HS(G)83 HSE Books 1992 ISBN 0 11 886316 9.

Woodworking Machines Regulations 1974. Guidance on Regulations L4 HSE Books 1991 ISBN 011 885592.

Work Equipment. Provision and Use of Work Equipment Regulations 1992. Guidance on Regulations L22 HSE Books 1992 ISBN 0 7176 0414 4.

INDEX